Alfred's
Teach Your Child To Play Piano

Ages 5 and Up

Christine H. Barden • Gayle Kowalchyk • E. L. Lancaster

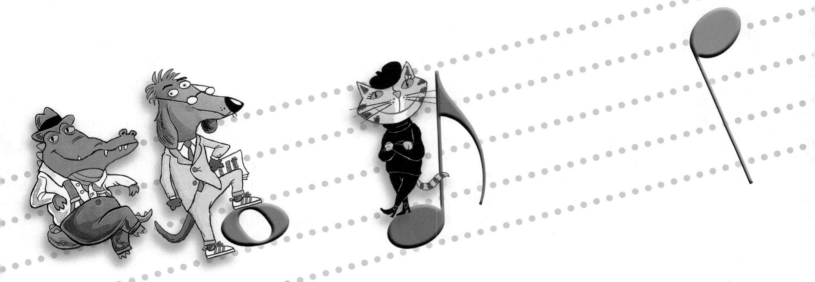

Alfred

Produced by
Alfred Music Publishing Co., Inc.
P.O. Box 10003
Van Nuys, CA 91410-0003
alfred.com

Copyright © 2013 by Alfred Music Publishing Co., Inc.
All rights reserved. Printed in USA.

ISBN-10: 0-7390-9470-X
ISBN-13: 978-0-7390-9470-9

Cover and interior illustrations by Jeff Shelly.

To the Parents

Playing the piano is one of the true joys of life. Music surrounds us in all aspects of our lives. Performing or listening to music brings pleasure and relaxation into busy daily schedules. It can help take away the cares and tensions of a troubled world. Consequently, many parents who studied piano want to share the gift of music with their children. They begin this process by teaching children the basics of piano before beginning formal study with a professional teacher.

About This Book

This book is designed for those parents and for homeschool families who wish to include piano in the curriculum. The step-by-step method provides materials that allow students to play pieces on the piano immediately. With an accompanying CD that demonstrates how the music sounds, each lesson is explained in plain language that is easy to understand.

Preceding each student page is a guide for parents. The guide suggests steps for introducing the concept or page to the student, follow-up practice suggestions, and suggestions for reviewing the page in subsequent lessons. To aid with planning, some pages have space where parents can write notes relating to the lesson.

About the Recording

The enclosed CD contains a recording of every piece in the book. Listening or playing along with the recording is fun, but more importantly, it can reinforce musical concepts such as rhythm, dynamics, and phrasing.

A CD icon (💿) beside the title of each song shows two track numbers. The first track number is for the student part alone, and the second track number is for the student part with a colorful accompaniment. For convenience, you may download the CD onto an MP3 player, digital music player, or iPod.

About the Lessons

Parents should set aside a regular lesson time each week for the child and strictly adhere to this schedule. Some parents even have children go outside, ring the doorbell, and enter the house to begin the lessons. This ensures that students know that the lessons are a special time that is separate from other family activities.

Parents who have a good background in music can teach piano basics effectively, but at some point children will need a professional teacher to continue their studies. Another teacher should be sought when the materials are beyond the understanding of the parent or at a point when lessons create tensions that jeopardize the parent-child relationship.

Page 96 contains some frequently asked questions about teaching your child. Good luck as you begin an exciting musical journey together!

Contents

How to Sit at the Piano

Posture at the piano is very important. It gives the pianist freedom to move around the keyboard and to pedal correctly. Your child should always have good posture when playing the piano.

Introducing the Concept

Discuss the information on page 5 with your child and do the suggested activities.

1. Adjust the bench squarely in front of the piano before sitting on it.
2. Sit in the middle of the bench with the body on the front half of the bench.
3. Make sure that the bench is the correct distance from the piano. To find the correct distance, extend the arms straight out away from the body. The back of the hands should touch the fallboard.
4. Feet should be flat on the floor if the legs are long enough. If not, place a bench or book under the feet.
5. Sit tall with the arms hanging loosely from the shoulders.

Practice Suggestions

1. Check your child's posture every time he or she sits at the piano.
2. Recheck his or her posture before each piece.

Subsequent Lessons

Don't worry if you have to keep reminding your child about posture. This is an ongoing skill that will require work for quite some time.

Curve Your Fingers!

Your child's fingers should always be curved when he or she is playing. This is something you will need to remind him or her about frequently. It should look as if he or she is holding a bubble in the hand.

Introducing the Concept

1. Use a small ball for your child to hold and wrap his or her fingers around. This will show how the fingers should be curved.
2. Place the student's hands on the keyboard. Tell the child to gently expand the fingers until each tip is touching a key. Be sure the fingers are curved. The palm of the hand should not be touching the keyboard.

Practice Suggestions

1. Close the cover of the keyboard. Have your child place the right hand on the cover with the fingers curved.
2. Keeping the fingers curved, have your child gently "pull" his or her finger tips back, keeping the palm of the hand off the cover.
3. Repeat with the left hand.

Subsequent Lessons

Curving the fingers, also known as "hand position," is a skill that takes a long time to develop. You will need to keep reminding your child to keep the fingers curved.

How to Sit at the Piano

To play well, it is important to sit correctly at the piano. Follow the instructions on this page so you are playing with good posture and hand position. You will also learn to sit at the correct height on the bench and at the right distance from the keyboard.

- Sit tall!
- Let your arms hang loosely from your shoulders.
- Place the bench facing the piano squarely.

If you are small:
Sit on a book or cushion.

If your feet don't touch the floor:
Place a book or stool under your feet.

Curve Your Fingers!

Always curve your fingers when you play.
1. Practice pretending to hold a bubble in your hand.
2. Shape your hand and hold the bubble gently so that it doesn't pop.
3. Use this hand position on the keyboard.

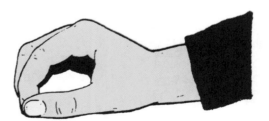

Left Hand Finger Numbers

Each finger is numbered for ease in playing the piano.

The thumb is finger 1 in each hand.

Then the fingers are numbered consecutively.

The pinky is finger 5.

Introducing the Concept

Discuss the information on page 7 with your child and do the suggested activities.

1. Have your child hold up the left hand.
   Point to each finger and say the corresponding finger number.

2. Repeat, but this time as you point to each finger, ask your child to say the finger number.

3. Have your child point to each finger of the left hand with the right hand and say the finger number.

Practice Suggestions

1. Have your child trace an outline of the left hand on a separate piece of paper.
   Then number each finger.

2. Have your child hold up the left hand.
   As you call out different finger numbers, have him or her wiggle the fingers that you name.

Subsequent Lessons

Review finger numbers as needed using the activities listed above.

Notes:

Left Hand Finger Numbers

Fingers are given numbers for playing the piano.
The thumb is finger 1, and the pinky is finger 5.
Memorize the numbers of all your fingers.

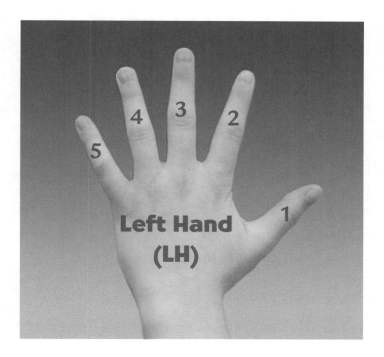

Hold up your left hand and wiggle each finger:
- Finger 1 (Thumbkin)
- Finger 2 (Pointer)
- Finger 3 (Tall Man)
- Finger 4 (Ring Man)
- Finger 5 (Pinky)

Activity

Draw an outline of your left hand in the space below and number each finger.

Right Hand Finger Numbers

The fingers of the right hand are numbered the same way as the left hand.

Introducing the Concept

Discuss the information on page 9 with your child and do the suggested activities.

1. Have your child hold up the right hand.
   Point to each finger and say the corresponding finger number.

2. Repeat, but this time as you point to each finger,
   ask your child to say the finger number.

3. Have your child point to each finger of the right hand
   with the left hand and say the finger number.

Practice Suggestions

1. Have your child trace an outline of the right hand on
   a separate piece of paper.
   Then number each finger.

2. Have your child hold up the right hand.
   As you call out different finger numbers,
   have him or her wiggle the fingers that you name.

3. Have your child put the hands together with palms facing in.
   As you call out different finger numbers,
   have him or her tap together the fingers that you name.

Subsequent Lessons

Review finger numbers as needed using the activities listed above.

Notes:

Right Hand Finger Numbers

The fingers of the right hand are numbered the same way as the left hand. Put your hands together, with fingers touching, and steadily tap finger 1 of both hands against each other. Then tap together finger 2 of both hands, then finger 3, finger 4, and finger 5.

Hold up your **right hand** and wiggle each finger:

* Finger 1 (Thumbkin)
* Finger 2 (Pointer)
* Finger 3 (Tall Man)
* Finger 4 (Ring Man)
* Finger 5 (Pinky)

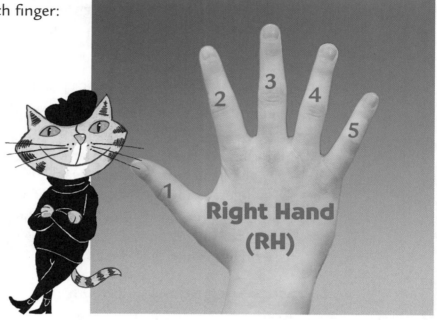

Activity

Draw an outline of your right hand in the space below and number each finger.

The Keyboard

The keyboard consists of white and black keys. The keys on the left side make low sounds, and the keys on the right side make high sounds. As you play the keys in the middle of the keyboard and move to the left (DOWN), you will notice that the sounds get lower. As you play the keys in the middle of the keyboard and move to the right (UP), you will notice that the sounds get higher.

Two-Black-Key Groups

Without the black keys, it would be impossible to tell which white key to play. The black keys are divided into groups of twos and threes. For now, your child will play the two-black-key groups with fingers 2 and 3 in each hand.

Introducing the Page

Discuss the information on page 11 with your child and do the suggested activities.

1. Find and play all of the two-black-key groups on the keyboard. Use fingers 2 and 3 of either hand.

2. Find the group of two black keys in the middle of the keyboard. Play all of the groups of two black keys going UP the keyboard. Use fingers 2 and 3 of the right hand.

3. Find the group of two black keys in the middle of the keyboard. Play all of the groups of two black keys going DOWN the keyboard. Use fingers 2 and 3 of the left hand.

Practice Suggestions

1. Review #2 and #3 from above.

2. Play two-black-key groups in different areas of the keyboard— high, middle, and low.

Subsequent Lessons

1. Trade places with your child. Ask him or her to close the eyes. Play a group of two black keys anywhere on the keyboard. Ask your child to identify whether it is high or low. Repeat several times.

2. Play groups of two black keys going UP the keyboard. Ask your child to identify whether they go up or down.

3. Play groups of two black keys going DOWN on the keyboard. Ask your child to identify whether they go up or down.

Notes:

The Keyboard

The keyboard has white keys and black keys.
The keys on the left side of the keyboard make low sounds.
The keys on the right make high sounds.

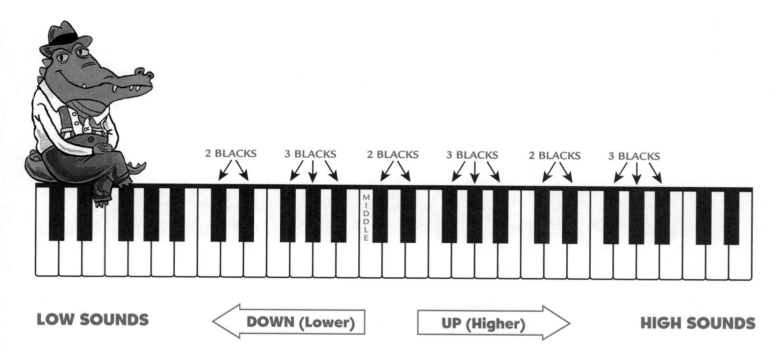

2 BLACKS   3 BLACKS   2 BLACKS   3 BLACKS   2 BLACKS   3 BLACKS

MIDDLE

LOW SOUNDS   ← DOWN (Lower)   UP (Higher) →   HIGH SOUNDS

Two-Black-Key Groups

Two-black-key groups are easy to find.
Count the number of two-black-key groups on your keyboard.

LH

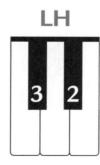

Using LH fingers 2 and 3 together, begin at the middle of the keyboard and play both notes of each two-black-key group going down to the bottom of the keyboard.

Do the sounds get **higher** or **lower**?

RH

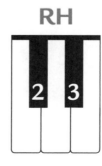

Using RH fingers 2 and 3 together, begin at the middle of the keyboard and play both notes of each two-black-key group going up to the top of the keyboard.

Do the sounds get **higher** or **lower**?

Parent Guide

Three-Black-Key-Groups

Groups of three black keys alternate with groups of two black keys. Your child will play the three-black-key groups with fingers 2, 3, and 4 in each hand.

Introducing the Page

Discuss the information on page 13 with your child and do the suggested activities.

1. Find and play all of the three-black-key groups on the keyboard.
   Use fingers 2, 3, and 4 of either hand.

2. Find the group of three black keys in the middle of the keyboard.
   Play all of the groups of three black keys going UP the keyboard.
   Use fingers 2, 3, and 4 of the right hand.

3. Find the group of three black keys in the middle of the keyboard.
   Play all of the groups of three black keys going DOWN the keyboard.
   Use fingers 2, 3, and 4 of the left hand.

4. Trade places with your child. Ask him or her to close the eyes.
   Play groups of three black keys going up or down the keyboard.
   Ask your child to identify whether they go up or down.
   Repeat several times.

Practice Suggestions

1. Review #2 and #3 from above.

2. Play three-black-key groups in different areas of the keyboard—
   high, middle, and low.

Subsequent Lessons

1. Trade places with your child. Ask him or her to close the eyes.
   Play a group of three black keys anywhere on the keyboard.
   Ask your child to identify whether it is high or low.
   Repeat several times.

2. Play groups of three black keys going UP the keyboard.
   Ask your child to identify whether they go up or down.

3. Play groups of three black keys going DOWN on the keyboard.
   Ask your child to identify whether they go up or down.

Notes:

Three-Black-Key Groups

Three-black-key groups alternate with two-black-key groups.
Count the number of three-black-key groups on your keyboard.

LH

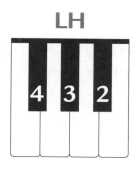

Using LH fingers 2, 3, and 4 together, begin at the middle of the keyboard and play all three notes of each three-black-key group going down to the bottom of the keyboard.

Do the sounds get **higher** or **lower**?

RH

Using RH fingers 2, 3, and 4 together, begin at the middle of the keyboard and play all three notes of each three-black-key group going up to the top of the keyboard.

Do the sounds get **higher** or **lower**?

Activity

1. Circle each group of two black keys.
2. Draw a box around each group of three black keys.

Playing Two Black Keys

Now your child is ready to play loud and soft sounds on two black keys.
The symbols for these sounds are called dynamics, and they are abbreviations for
Italian words. To play loudly (*f* or *forte*), your child will need to use the weight of
the arm. To play softly, (*p* or *piano*) he or she will use less arm weight.

Introducing the Page

Discuss the information on page 15 with your child and do the suggested activities.

1. Play all of the two-black-key groups on the entire keyboard loudly.
   Use fingers 2 and 3 of either hand.
2. Play all of the two-black-key groups on the entire keyboard softly.
   Use fingers 2 and 3 of either hand.

Practice Suggestions

1. Play two low black keys loudly, and then play them again softly.
   Use the left hand.
2. Play two high black keys softly, and then play them again loudly.
   Use the right hand.

Subsequent Lessons

1. Talk about the things in your house that make noise.
   Decide if the noise each one makes is loud (*f*) or soft (*p*).
2. Continue to review the groups of two black keys in the following ways:
   - Going up
   - Going down
   - High
   - Low
   - Loud
   - Soft

Notes:

Playing Two Black Keys

Symbols that show how loud or soft to play are called *dynamics*.
These symbols come from Italian words.

Loud Sounds

f

The sign *f* stands for *forte,*
which means to play **loud.**

Using LH fingers 2 and 3, play two black keys
low on the keyboard at once. Play the two keys
loudly (*f*) on each word as you say,

"I can play two low black keys."

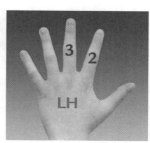

Soft Sounds

p

The sign *p* stands for *piano,*
which means to play **soft.**

Using RH fingers 2 and 3, play two black keys
high on the keyboard at once. Play the two keys
softly (*p*) on each word as you say,

"I can play two high black keys."

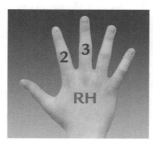

Using fingers 2 and 3 of either hand, play **all** the
two-black-key groups on the entire keyboard.

Quarter Note

Notes tell how long sounds last. Notes are used to indicate rhythm, which is the pulse of music. A quarter note is made of a note head (the black circle) and the stem (the straight line). A quarter note gets one count. Notes with the stems going up on the right are played by the right hand. Notes with stems going down on the left are played by the left hand.

Introducing the Page

Discuss the information on page 17 with your child and do the suggested activities.

For each piece on the page, follow these steps with your child:

1. Tap the rhythm on the lap. Use the correct hand and count aloud, saying "1 1 1 1."
2. "Play" the piece on the closed keyboard cover and say the finger numbers aloud.
3. Play the piece on the keyboard and count aloud.
4. Play and sing the words.

Practice Suggestions

1. Point to the quarter notes in the pieces and count aloud evenly.
2. Play one key at a time and say the finger numbers.
3. Play and sing the words.

Subsequent Lessons

1. Review *Right Hand Marching* and *Left Hand Marching* as needed. Work for a steady tempo. Remember the dynamics.
2. Play *Right Hand Marching* and *Left Hand Marching* with the CD.

Notes:

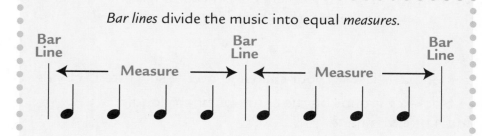
Quarter Note

Bar lines divide the music into equal *measures*.

Bar Line   Bar Line   Bar Line

←——— Measure ———→ ←——— Measure ———→

Introducing the Quarter Note

Each quarter note has a black circle called a *notehead* with a line called a *stem*.

notehead

stem

A *quarter note* gets **one** count.

Count: 1   1   1   1

Practice Directions

Now it is time to play your first pieces on the keyboard. Follow these practice directions.

1. Point to the quarter notes in the songs below and count aloud evenly.
2. Play one key at a time and say the finger numbers.
3. Play and sing the words.

Right Hand Marching

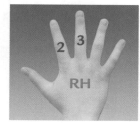

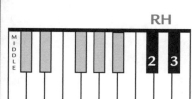

Track 1 (45)

RH

f

DOUBLE BAR
used at the end

	2	3	2	3		2	3	2	3	
Count:	1	1	1	1		1	1	1	1	
	Right	hand	march	- ing,		2	3	2	3.	

Left Hand Walking

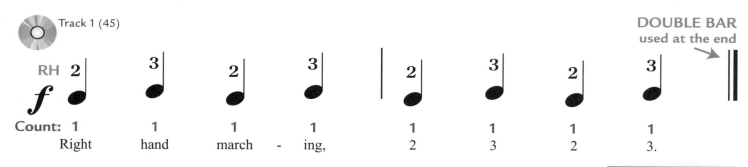

Track 2 (46)

p

LH

2	3	2	3		2	3	2	3	
Count: 1	1	1	1		1	1	1	1
Left	hand	walk	- ing,		2	3	2	3.

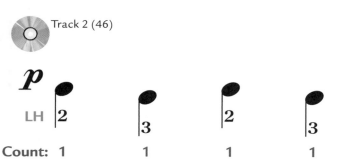

Playing Three Black Keys

Now your child is ready to play loud and soft sounds on three black keys. The symbols for these sounds are called dynamics, and they are abbreviations for Italian words. To play loudly (f or *forte*), your child will need to use the weight of the arm. To play softly, (p or *piano*) he or she will use less arm weight.

Introducing the Page

Discuss the information on page 19 with your child and do the suggested activities.

1. Play all of the three-black-key groups on the entire keyboard loudly. Use fingers 2, 3, and 4 of either hand.

2. Play all of the three-black-key groups on the entire keyboard softly. Use fingers 2, 3, and 4 of either hand.

Practice Suggestions

1. Play three low black keys loudly, and then play them again softly. Use the left hand.

2. Play three high black keys softly, and then play them again loudly. Use the right hand.

Subsequent Lessons

Continue to review the groups of three black keys in the following ways:
- Going up
- Going down
- High
- Low
- Loud
- Soft

Notes:

Playing Three Black Keys

When playing the three black keys, remember to play loud for f and soft for p.

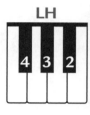 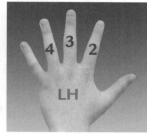

Using LH fingers 2, 3, and 4, play three black keys **low** on the keyboard at once. Play the three keys softly (p) on each word as you say,

"I can play three low black keys."

Using RH fingers 2, 3, and 4, play three black keys **high** on the keyboard at once. Play the three keys loudly (f) on each word as you say,

"I can play three high black keys."

Using fingers 2, 3, and 4 of either hand, play **all** the three-black-key groups on the entire keyboard.

Quarter Rest

Rests are signs of silence. Rests tell you when to lift your hand so that the sound will stop. Every note has a corresponding rest that has the same value. Rests are counted just as notes are counted. A quarter rest, like the quarter note, gets one count. Here, your child will say the word "rest" for each quarter rest.

Introducing the Page

Discuss the information on page 21 with your child and do the suggested activities.

For each piece on the page, follow these steps with your child:

1. Tap the rhythm on the lap. Use the correct hand and count aloud, saying "1 1 1 rest." For the rest, have your child lift the hand and turn the palm up while saying "rest."
2. "Play" the piece on the closed keyboard cover and say the finger numbers aloud. For the rest, have your child lift the finger off the closed keyboard.
3. Play the piece on the keyboard and count aloud. For the rest, have your child lift the finger off the keyboard.
4. Play and sing the words.

Practice Suggestions

1. Point to the quarter notes and quarter rests and count aloud evenly.
2. Clap and count the rhythms aloud.
3. Play and say the finger numbers.
4. Play and sing the words.

Subsequent Lessons

1. Continue practicing *A Mouse's Melody* and *A Bear's Song* as needed.
2. Play *A Mouse's Melody* and *A Bear's Song* with the CD.

Notes:

Quarter Rest

Introducing the Quarter Rest

Rests are signs of **silence.** They tell you to lift your hand to stop the sound.

A quarter rest

𝄽

gets **one** count.

Practice Directions

1. Point to the quarter notes and quarter rests and count aloud evenly.
2. Clap and count the rhythms aloud.
3. Play and say the finger numbers.
4. Play and sing the words.

A Mouse's Melody Track 3 (47)

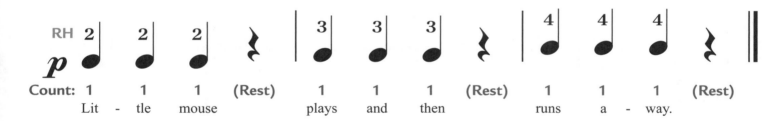

RH

p

Count: 1   1   1   (Rest)   1   1   1   (Rest)   1   1   1   (Rest)

Lit - tle mouse   plays and then   runs a - way.

A Bear's Song Track 4 (48)

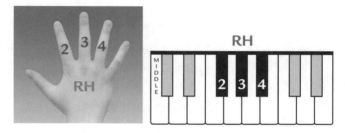

f

LH

Count: 1   1   1   (Rest)   1   1   1   (Rest)   1   1   1   (Rest)

My bear's song   is not long.   Now it's gone.

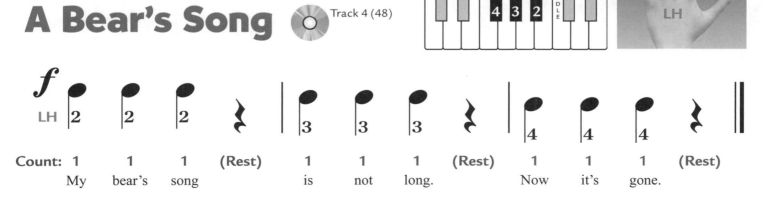

Half Note

One half note is equal to two quarter notes. A half note gets two counts.

Introducing the Page

Discuss the information on page 23 with your child and do the suggested activities.

For *Hot Cross Buns,* follow these steps with your child:

1. Clap the rhythm. For the half notes, have your child clap on "1" then squeeze the hands together and shake them once on "2."

2. Next, tap the rhythm on the lap. This is the first piece your child has played that has two lines of music. The first line is for the right hand, and the second line is for the left hand.

3. "Play" the piece on the closed keyboard cover and say the finger numbers aloud.

4. Play the piece on the keyboard and count aloud.

5. Play and sing the words.

Practice Suggestions

1. Point to the quarter notes and half notes and count aloud evenly.

2. Clap and count the rhythms aloud.

3. Play and say the finger numbers.

4. Play and sing the words.

Subsequent Lessons

1. Review *Hot Cross Buns* as needed.

2. Change the dynamics. Play the entire piece *p (piano)*. Next play the right hand *f (forte)* and the left hand *p* . Then switch the dynamics so that the right hand is *p* and the left hand is *f*.

3. *Play Hot Cross Buns* with the CD.

4. If desired, your child can play *Hot Cross Buns* hands together (right hand and left hand play at the same time).

Notes:

Half Note

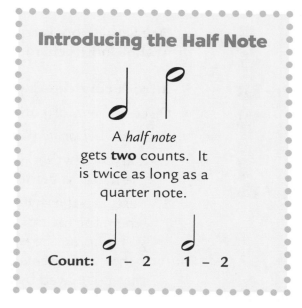

Introducing the Half Note

A *half note* gets **two** counts. It is twice as long as a quarter note.

Count: 1 – 2   1 – 2

Practice Directions

1. Point to the quarter notes and half notes and count aloud evenly.
2. Clap and count the rhythms aloud.
3. Play and say the finger numbers.
4. Play and sing the words.

The right hand plays the top line, and the left hand plays the bottom line.

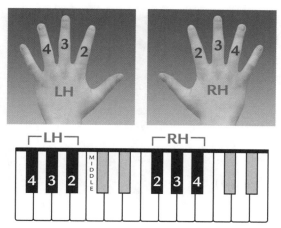

Hot Cross Buns

Track 5 (49)

RH

f

Count: 1   1   1 – 2   1   1   1 – 2   1   1   1   1   1   1   1 – 2
Hot cross buns!   Hot cross buns!   Yum - my, yum - my,   hot cross buns!

LH

Count: 1   1   1 – 2   1   1   1 – 2   1   1   1   1   1   1   1 – 2
Hot cross buns!   Hot cross buns!   Yum - my, yum - my,   hot cross buns!

23

Whole Note

One whole note is equal to four quarter notes or two half notes.
A whole note gets four counts.

Introducing the Page

Discuss the information on page 25 with your child and do the suggested activities.

For *Old MacDonald Had a Farm,* follow these steps with your child:

1. Clap the rhythm. For the whole notes, have your child clap on "1" then squeeze the hands together and shake them once on each following count "2," "3," "4."

2. Next, tap the rhythm on the lap. This is the first piece your child has played where the melody line is divided between the two hands. Remember that stems going up on the right side of the note head indicate notes that are played by the right hand. Stems going down on the left side of the note head indicate notes that are played by the left hand.

3. "Play" the piece on the closed keyboard cover and say the finger numbers aloud.

4. Play the piece on the keyboard and count aloud.

5. Play and sing the words aloud.

Practice Suggestions

1. Point to the notes and count aloud evenly.

2. Clap and count the rhythms aloud.

3. Play and say the finger numbers.

4. Play and sing the words.

Subsequent Lessons

1. Review *Old MacDonald Had a Farm* as needed.

2. Change the dynamics. Play the entire piece *p (piano)*.

3. Play *Old MacDonald Had a Farm* with the CD.

Notes:

Whole Note

Introducing the Whole Note

𝆶

A *whole note* gets **four** counts. It is as long as two half notes or four quarter notes.

Count: 1 – 2 – 3 – 4

Practice Directions

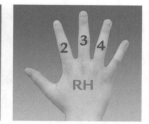

1. Point to the notes and count aloud evenly.
2. Clap and count the rhythms aloud.
3. Play and say the finger numbers.
4. Play and sing the words.

The right hand alternates with the left hand on each line.

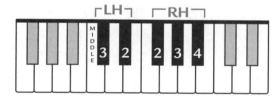

Old MacDonald Had a Farm 💿 Track 6 (50)

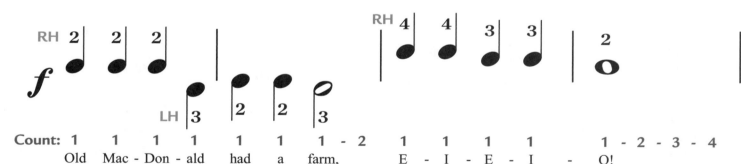

Count: 1   1   1   1   1   1   1 - 2   1   1   1   1   1 - 2 - 3 - 4
Old Mac - Don - ald had   a farm,   E - I - E - I - O!

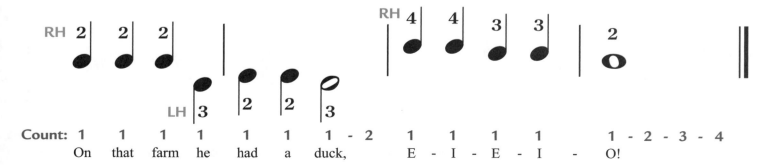

Count: 1   1   1   1   1   1   1 - 2   1   1   1   1   1 - 2 - 3 - 4
On that farm he had   a duck,   E - I - E - I - O!

25

White Keys

The white keys are named using the first seven letters of the alphabet.
This is called the music alphabet. A is the lowest key on the keyboard.
The keys are named consecutively. Once you reach G, you start over again with A.

Introducing the Page

Discuss the information on page 27 with your child
and do the suggested activities.

Start with the lowest key on the keyboard.
Play and name each key aloud going up.

Practice Suggestions

1. Say the music alphabet forward and backward.
2. Begin on different letters and say the music alphabet forward and backward.
3. Start with the lowest key on the keyboard.
   Play and name each key aloud going up.
4. Start with the highest key on the keyboard.
   Play and name each key aloud going down.

Subsequent Lessons

1. Make a set of music alphabet flashcards with one letter (A–G) on each card.
2. Begin with A and place the cards in order going up.
3. Begin with G and place the cards in order going down.
4. Begin with different cards and go up or down.

Notes:

White Keys

The white keys are named for the first seven letters of the alphabet:

A B C D E F G

The lowest key on the
keyboard is A.

The highest key on the
keyboard is C.

A B C D E F G A B C D E F G A B C D E F G A B C D E F G A B C D E F G A B C D E F G A B C D E F G A B C

LOW

Middle C

HIGH

Did You Notice?

The key names are used
over and over!

Write the name of each white key on the keyboard below.

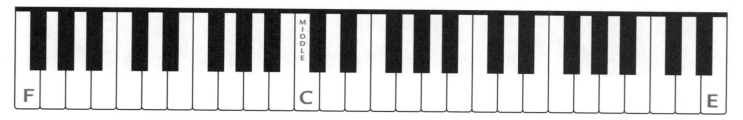

F

C

E

Finding D on the Keyboard

D is the easiest white key to find on the keyboard. It is the white key located in the middle of the two black keys.

Introducing the Page

Discuss the information on page 29 with your child and do the suggested activities.

Have your child find and play all of the D's on the keyboard.

For *The D Song,* follow these steps:

1. Clap the rhythm. Your child should turn the palms up for each quarter rest.
2. "Play" the piece on the closed keyboard cover with RH finger 2.
3. Play the piece on the keyboard and count aloud.
4. Play and sing the words.

Practice Suggestions

1. Clap (or tap) and count aloud evenly.
2. Point to the notes and rests and count aloud evenly.
3. Play and sing the words.

Subsequent Lessons

Play the following on the keyboard:

1. Starting with the lowest D, play all of the D's going up.
2. Starting with the highest D, play all of the D's going down.
3. Play a D in the middle.
4. Play a high D.
5. Play a low D.
6. Review *The D Song* as needed.
7. Play *The D Song* with the CD.

Notes:

Finding D on the Keyboard

D is the white key in the middle of a two-black-key group.

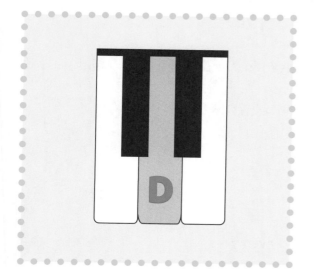

Find each D on the keyboard below and color it yellow.

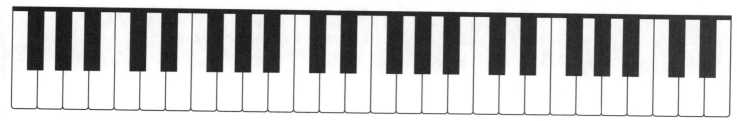

Practice Directions

Use finger 2 (Pointer) to play each D in *The D Song*.

1. Clap (or tap) and count aloud evenly.
2. Point to the notes and rests and count aloud evenly.
3. Play and sing the words.

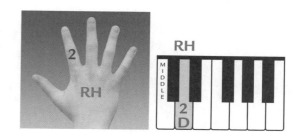

The D Song Track 7 (51)

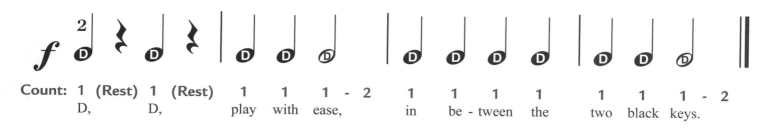

Count:	1	(Rest)	1	(Rest)	1	1	1 - 2	1	1	1	1	1	1	1 - 2
	D,		D,		play	with	ease,	in	be - tween	the		two	black	keys.

29

Finding C on the Keyboard

C is the white key to the left of a two-black-key group. It is to the left of D.

Introducing the Page

Discuss the information on page 31 with your child and do the suggested activities. Have your child find and play all of the C's on the keyboard.

For *The C Song,* follow these steps:

1. Clap the rhythm. (This is the same rhythm used in *The D Song.*) Your child should turn the palms up for each quarter rest.
2. "Play" the piece on the closed keyboard cover with RH finger 1.
3. Play the piece on the keyboard and count aloud.
4. Play and sing the words aloud.

Practice Suggestions

1. Clap (or tap) and count aloud evenly.
2. Point to the notes and rests and count aloud evenly.
3. Play and sing the words.

Subsequent Lessons

Play the following on the keyboard:

1. Starting with the lowest C, play all of the C's going up.
2. Starting with the highest C, play all of the C's going down.
3. Play a C in the middle.
4. Play a high C.
5. Play a low C.
6. Use the music alphabet flash cards to review the music alphabet.
7. Review *The C Song* as needed.
8. Play *The C Song* with the CD.

Notes:

Finding C on the Keyboard

C is the white key to the left of a two-black-key group.

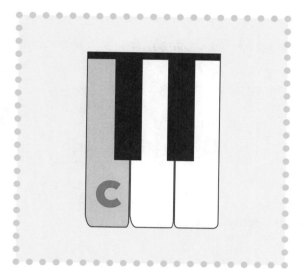

Find each C on the keyboard below and color it green.

Practice Directions

Use finger 1 (Thumbkin) to play each C in *The C Song*.

1. Clap (or tap) and count aloud evenly.
2. Point to the notes and rests and count aloud evenly.
3. Play and sing the words.

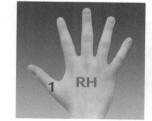

The C Song Track 8 (52)

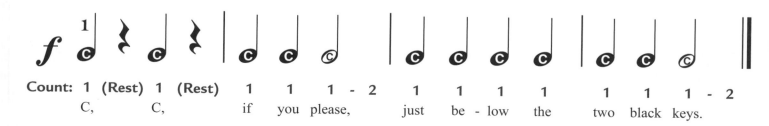

Count:	1	(Rest)	1	(Rest)	1	1	1 - 2	1	1	1	1	1	1	1 - 2
	C,		C,		if	you	please,	just	be - low	the		two	black	keys.

Finding E on the Keyboard

E is the white key to the right of a two-black-key group. It is to the right of D.

Introducing the Page

Discuss the information on page 33 with your child and do the suggested activities. Have your child find and play all of the E's on the keyboard.

For *The E Song*, follow these steps with your child:

1. Clap the rhythm. (This is the same rhythm used in *The D Song*.) Your child should turn the palms up for each quarter rest.
2. "Play" the piece on the closed keyboard cover with RH finger 3.
3. Play the piece on the keyboard and count aloud.
4. Play and sing the words.

Practice Suggestions

1. Clap (or tap) and count aloud evenly.
2. Point to the notes and rests and count aloud evenly.
3. Play and sing the words.

Subsequent Lessons

Play the following on the keyboard:

1. Starting with the lowest E, play all of the E's going up.
2. Starting with the highest E, play all of the E's going down.
3. Play an E in the middle.
4. Play a high E.
5. Play a low E.
6. Review the music alphabet as needed.
7. Review *The E Song* as needed.
8. Play *The E Song* with the CD.

Notes:

Finding E on the Keyboard

E is the white key to the right of a two-black-key group.

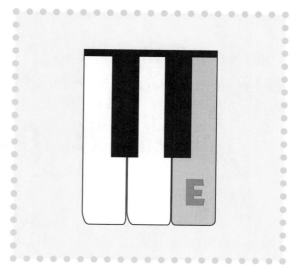

Find each E on the keyboard below and color it red.

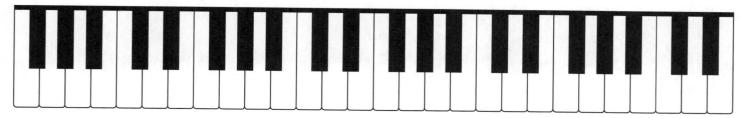

Practice Directions

Use finger 3 (Tall Man) to play each E in *The E Song*.

1. Clap (or tap) and count aloud evenly.
2. Point to the notes and rests and count aloud evenly.
3. Play and sing the words.

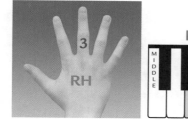

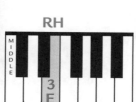

The E Song ◎ Track 9 (53)

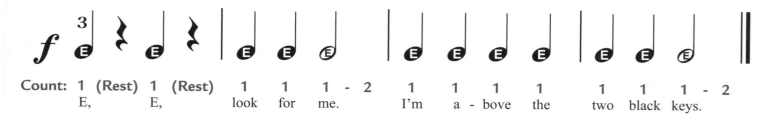

Count: 1 (Rest) 1 (Rest)   1   1   1 - 2   1   1   1   1   1   1   1 - 2
    E,   E,   look for me.   I'm a - bove the   two black keys.

33

Go Tell Aunt Rhody (for RH)

Go Tell Aunt Rhody (for RH) uses the three white keys (C, D, E) that your child has learned.

Introducing the Page

Find and play all of the C-D-E groups on the keyboard using fingers 1, 2, and 3 of the right hand. These are the three white keys that surround the two-black key groups.

For *Go Tell Aunt Rhody (for RH)*, follow these steps:

1. Clap the rhythm.
2. "Play" the piece on the closed keyboard cover and say the finger numbers aloud.
3. Play the piece on the keyboard and count aloud.
4. Play and sing the words aloud.

Practice Suggestions

1. Clap (or tap) and count aloud evenly.
2. Point to the notes and count aloud evenly.
3. Say the finger numbers aloud while playing the notes in the air.
4. Play and say the finger numbers.
5. Play and say the note names.
6. Play and sing the words.

Subsequent Lessons

Play the following on the keyboard:

1. Starting with the lowest C-D-E group, play all of the C-D-E's going up.
2. Starting with the highest C-D-E group, play all of the C-D-E's going down.
3. Play a C-D-E group in the middle.
4. Play a high C-D-E group.
5. Play a low C-D-E group.
6. Review *Go Tell Aunt Rhody (for RH)* as needed.
7. Play *Go Tell Aunt Rhody (for RH)* with CD.

Notes:

Practice Directions

1. Clap (or tap) and count aloud evenly.
2. Point to the notes and count aloud evenly.
3. Say the finger numbers aloud while playing the notes in the air.
4. Play and say the finger numbers.
5. Play and say the note names.
6. Play and sing the words.

"Go Tell Aunt Rhody" for right hand uses finger 1 on C, 2 on D, and 3 on E.

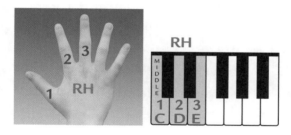

Go Tell Aunt Rhody (for RH) Track 10 (54)

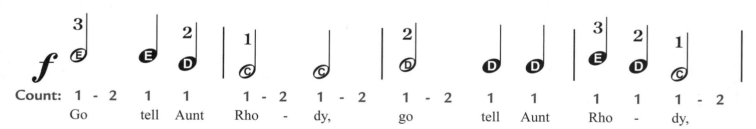

Count: 1 - 2   1   1   1 - 2   1 - 2   1 - 2   1   1   1   1   1 - 2
Go   tell Aunt Rho   -   dy,   go   tell   Aunt   Rho   -   dy,

Skip 2 on D

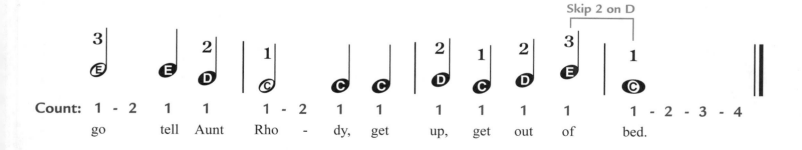

Count: 1 - 2   1   1   1 - 2   1   1   1   1   1   1   1 - 2 - 3 - 4
go   tell Aunt Rho   -   dy, get   up, get out of   bed.

35

Go Tell Aunt Rhody (for LH)

Go Tell Aunt Rhody (for LH) uses the three white keys (C, D, E)
that your child has learned.

Introducing the Page

Find and play all of the C-D-E groups on the keyboard with fingers 1, 2, and 3 of the
left hand. For *Go Tell Aunt Rhody (for LH),* follow these steps:

1. Clap the rhythm.
2. "Play" the piece on the closed keyboard cover and say the finger numbers aloud.
3. Play the piece on the keyboard and count aloud.
4. Play and sing the words.

Practice Suggestions

1. Clap (or tap) and count aloud evenly.
2. Point to the notes and count aloud evenly.
3. Say the finger numbers aloud while playing the notes in the air.
4. Play and say the finger numbers.
5. Play and say the note names.
6. Play and sing the words.

Subsequent Lessons

Play the following on the keyboard:

1. Starting with the lowest C-D-E group, play all of the C-D-E's going up.
2. Starting with the highest C-D-E group, play all of the C-D-E's going down.
3. Play a C-D-E group in the middle.
4. Play a high C-D-E group.
5. Play a low C-D-E group.
6. Review *Go Tell Aunt Rhody (for LH)* as needed.
7. Play *Go Tell Aunt Rhody (for LH)* with the CD.

Notes:

Practice Directions

1. Clap (or tap) and count aloud evenly.
2. Point to the notes and count aloud evenly.
3. Say the finger numbers aloud while playing the notes in the air.
4. Play and say the finger numbers.
5. Play and say the note names.
6. Play and sing the words.

After you have learned to play "Go Tell Aunt Rhody" on both pages 35 and 37, play them without stopping in between to create a longer song.

"Go Tell Aunt Rhody" for left hand uses finger 3 on C, 2 on D, and 1 on E.

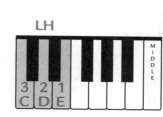 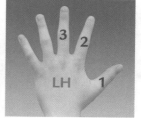

Go Tell Aunt Rhody (for LH) 🔘 Track 11 (55)

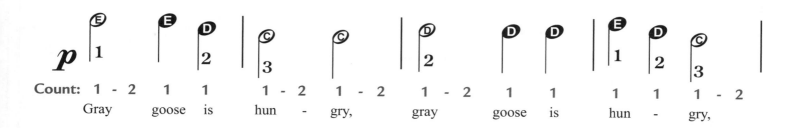

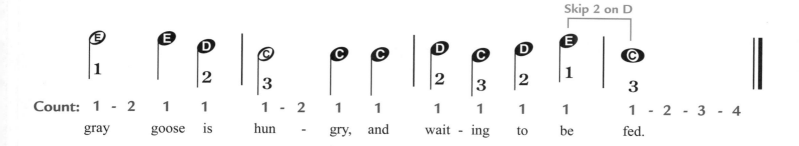

Review: C, D, E

Introducing the Page

Do the suggested activity at the top of page 39.

Review C, D, and E on the keyboard. Play high and low C's, D's, and E's.

The C Song, Again! is exactly like *The C Song* except that it is played with the left hand. For *The C Song, Again!* follow these steps:

1. Clap the rhythm. You child should turn the palms up for each quarter rest.
2. "Play" the piece on the closed keyboard cover with LH finger 1.
3. Play the piece on the keyboard and count aloud.
4. Play and sing the words aloud.

Practice Suggestions

1. Clap (or tap) and count aloud evenly.
2. Point to the notes and rests and count aloud evenly.
3. Play and sing the words.

Subsequent Lessons

Play the following on the keyboard:

1. Starting with the lowest C, play all of the C's going up.
2. Starting with the highest C, play all of the C's going down.
3. Play a C in the middle.
4. Play a high C.
5. Play a low C.
6. Review *The C Song, Again!* as needed.
7. Play *The C Song, Again!* with the CD.

Notes:

Review: C, D, E

Draw a line from each key marked with an "X" in the first column to its note name in the second column.

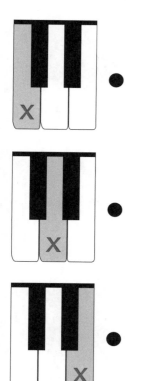

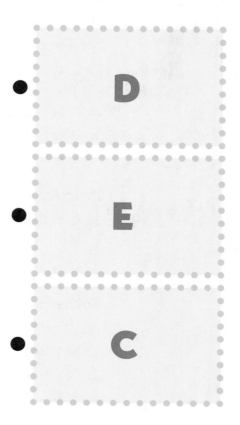

Practice Directions

Use left hand finger 1 (Thumbkin) to play each C in *The C Song, Again!*

1. Clap (or tap) and count aloud evenly.
2. Point to the notes and rests and count aloud evenly.
3. Play and sing the words.

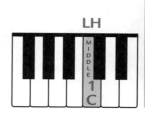 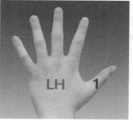

The C Song, Again! Track 12 (56)

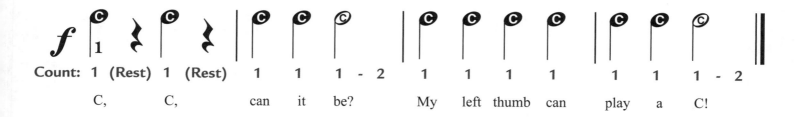

Count:	1	(Rest)	1	(Rest)	1	1	1 - 2	1	1	1	1	1	1	1 - 2
	C,		C,		can	it	be?	My	left	thumb	can	play	a	C!

Finding B on the Keyboard

B is to the right of a three-black key group.

Introducing the Page

Discuss the information on page 41 with your child and do the suggested activities.

Have you child find and play all of the B's on the keyboard.

For *The B Song,* follow these steps:

1. Clap the rhythm. (This is the same rhythm used in *The C Song, Again!*) Your child should turn the palms up for each quarter rest.
2. "Play" the piece on the closed keyboard cover with LH finger 2.
3. Play the piece on the keyboard and count aloud.
4. Play and sing the words aloud.

Practice Suggestions

1. Clap (or tap) and count aloud evenly.
2. Point to the notes and rests and count aloud evenly.
3. Play and sing the words.

Subsequent Lessons

Play the following on the keyboard:

1. Starting with the lowest B, play all of the B's going up.
2. Starting with the highest B, play all of the B's going down.
3. Play a B in the middle.
4. Play a high B.
5. Play a low B.
6. Review *The B Song* as needed.
7. Play *The B Song* with the CD.

Notes:

Finding B on the Keyboard

B is to the right of a three-black-key group.

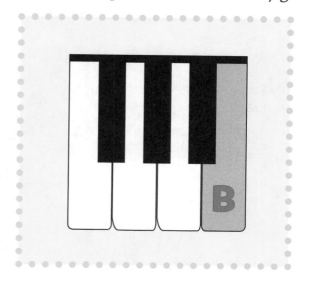

Find each B on the keyboard below and color it purple.

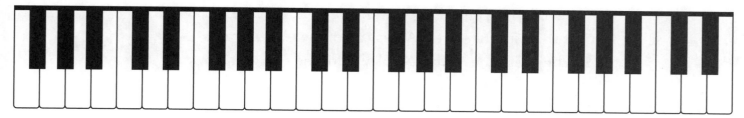

Practice Directions

Use left hand finger 2 (Pointer) to play each B in *The B Song*.

1. Clap (or tap) and count aloud evenly.
2. Point to the notes and rests and count aloud evenly.
3. Play and sing the words.

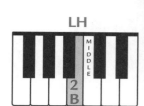

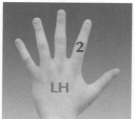

The B Song   Track 13 (57)

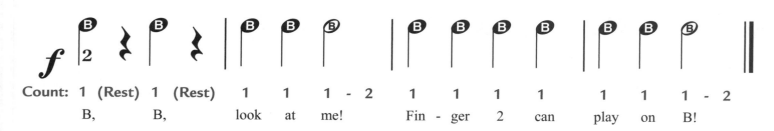

Count:	1	(Rest)	1	(Rest)	1	1	1 - 2	1	1	1	1	1	1	1 - 2
	B,		B,		look	at	me!	Fin	- ger	2	can	play	on	B!

Finding A on the Keyboard

A is the white key to the left of B. It is in between the middle and top (right) black keys of the three-black-key group.

Introducing the Page

Discuss the information on page 43 with your child and do the suggested activities.

Have your child find and play all of the A's on the keyboard.

For *The A Song,* follow these steps:

1. Clap the rhythm. (This is the same rhythm used in *The B Song.*) Your child should turn the palms up for each quarter rest.
2. "Play" the piece on the closed keyboard cover with LH finger 3.
3. Play the piece on the keyboard and count aloud.
4. Play and sing the words.

Practice Suggestions

1. Clap (or tap) and count aloud evenly.
2. Point to the notes and rests and count aloud evenly.
3. Play and sing the words.

Subsequent Lessons

Play the following on the keyboard:

1. Starting with the lowest A, play all of the A's going up.
2. Starting with the highest A, play all of the A's going down.
3. Play an A in the middle.
4. Play a high A.
5. Play a low A.
6. Review *The A Song* as needed.
7. Play *The A Song* with the CD.

Notes:

Finding A on the Keyboard

A is the white key to the left of B.

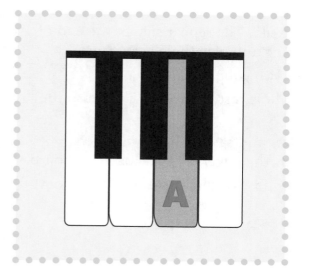

Find each A on the keyboard below and color it blue.

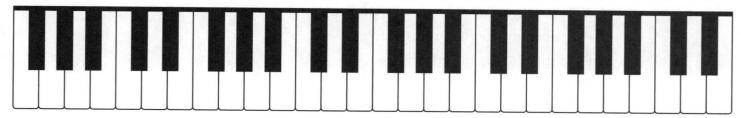

Practice Directions

Use left hand finger 3 (Tall Man) to play each A in *The A Song*.

1. Clap (or tap) and count aloud evenly.
2. Point to the notes and rests and count aloud evenly.
3. Play and sing the words.

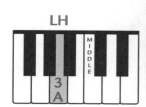

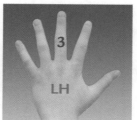

The A Song 🔘 Track 14 (58)

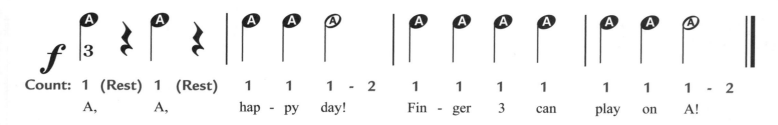

Count: 1 (Rest) 1 (Rest) 1   1   1 - 2   1   1   1   1   1   1   1 - 2
     A,   A,   hap - py day! Fin - ger 3   can   play on A!

Whole Rest

A whole rest is the corresponding rest to the whole note. It gets four counts and means to rest for the whole measure. Your child will count this rest saying "rest – 2 – 3 – 4," turning the palms up for the four counts.

Introducing the Page

Discuss the information on page 45 with your child. The repeat sign at the end of "Little Dance" means to go back to the beginning and play the piece again.

For each piece on the page, follow these steps with your child:

1. Clap the rhythm and count aloud. For the whole rest, have your child turn the palms up for the four counts.
2. "Play" the piece on the closed keyboard cover and say the finger numbers aloud. For the whole rest, have your child lift the finger off the closed keyboard.
3. Play the piece on the keyboard and count aloud. For the whole rest, have your child lift the finger off the keyboard.
4. Play and sing the words.

Practice Directions

1. Clap (or tap) and count aloud evenly.
2. Point to the notes and rests and count aloud evenly.
3. Say the finger numbers aloud while playing the notes in the air.
4. Play and say the finger numbers.
5. Play and say the note names.
6. Play and sing the words.

Subsequent Lessons

1. Review all of the A's, B's, and C's on the keyboard.
2. Review *Little Dance* and *Rainy Day* as needed.
3. Play *Little Dance* and *Rainy Day* with the CD.

Notes:

Whole Rest

Practice Directions

Remember to lift your hand for the whole rests as you play "Little Dance" and "Rainy Day."

1. Clap (or tap) and count aloud evenly.
2. Point to the notes and rests and count aloud evenly.
3. Say the finger numbers aloud while playing the notes in the air.
4. Play and say the finger numbers.
5. Play and say the note names.
6. Play and sing the words.

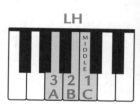

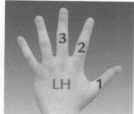

LH

REPEAT SIGN
Play again.

Little Dance — Track 15 (59)

f

Count: 1 1 1 - 2 Rest - 2 - 3 - 4 1 1 1 - 2 Rest - 2 - 3 - 4

Walk and stop. Walk and stop.

Rainy Day — Track 16 (60)

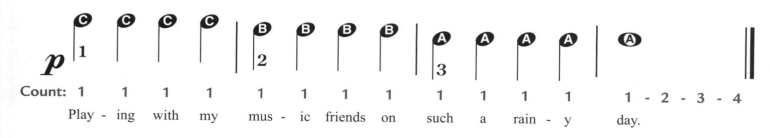

p

Count: 1 1 1 1 1 1 1 1 1 1 1 1 1 - 2 - 3 - 4

Play - ing with my mus - ic friends on such a rain - y day.

45

Finding F on the Keyboard

F is to the left of a three-black-key group. It is to the right of E.

Introducing the Page

Discuss the information on page 47 with your child and do the suggested activities.

Find and play all of the F's on the keyboard.

For *The F Song,* follow these steps with your child:

1. Clap the rhythm. (This is the same rhythm used in *The A Song.*)
   Your child should turn the palms up for each quarter rest.
2. "Play" the piece on the closed keyboard cover with RH finger 4.
3. Play the piece on the keyboard and count aloud.
4. Play and sing the words aloud.

Practice Suggestions

1. Clap (or tap) and count aloud evenly.
2. Point to the notes and rests and count aloud evenly.
3. Play and sing the words.

Subsequent Lessons

Play the following on the keyboard:

1. Starting with the lowest F, play all of the F's going up.
2. Starting with the highest F, play all of the F's going down.
3. Play an F in the middle.
4. Play a high F.
5. Play a low F.
6. Review *The F Song* as needed.
7. Play *The F Song* with the CD.

Notes:

Finding F on the Keyboard

F is to the left of a three-black-key group.

Find each F on the keyboard below and color it pink.

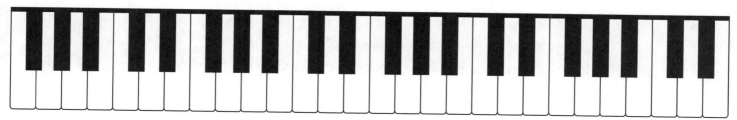

Practice Directions

Use right hand finger 4 (Ring Man) to play each F in *The F Song*.

1. Clap (or tap) and count aloud evenly.

2. Point to the notes and rests and count aloud evenly.

3. Play and sing the words.

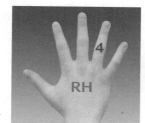 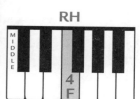

The F Song   Track 17 (61)

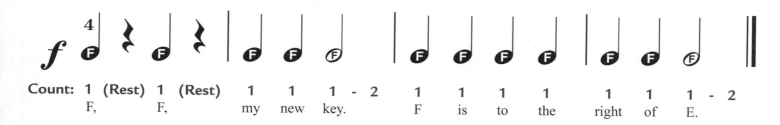

Count: 1 (Rest) 1 (Rest) 1 1 1 - 2 1 1 1 1 1 1 1 - 2
F, F, my new key. F is to the right of E.

Finding G on the Keyboard

G is the white key between F and A. It is in between the middle and bottom (left) black keys of the three-black-key group.

Introducing the Page

Discuss the information on page 49 with your child and do the suggested activities.

Find and play all of the G's on the keyboard.

For *The G Song*, follow these steps:

1. Clap the rhythm. (This is the same rhythm used in *The F Song*.) Your child should turn the palms up for each quarter rest.
2. "Play" the piece on the closed keyboard cover with RH finger 5.
3. Play the piece on the keyboard and count aloud.
4. Play and sing the words aloud.

Practice Suggestions

1. Clap (or tap) and count aloud evenly.
2. Point to the notes and rests and count aloud evenly.
3. Play and sing the words.

Subsequent Lessons

Play the following on the keyboard:

1. Starting with the lowest G, play all of the G's going up.
2. Starting with the highest G, play all of the G's going down.
3. Play a G in the middle.
4. Play a high G.
5. Play a low G.
6. Review the music alphabet with the alphabet cards.
7. Review *The G Song* as needed.
8. Play *The G Song* with the CD.

Notes:

Finding G on the Keyboard

G is the white key between F and A.

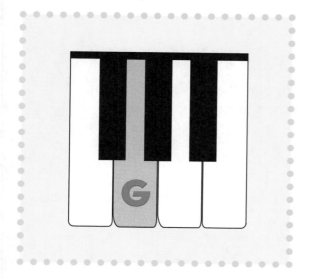

Find each G on the keyboard below and color it orange.

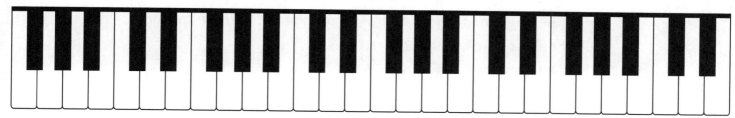

Practice Directions

Use right hand finger 5 (Pinky) to play each G in *The G Song*.

1. Clap (or tap) and count aloud evenly.
2. Point to the notes and rests and count aloud evenly.
3. Play and sing the words.

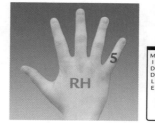
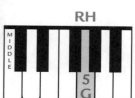

The G Song  Track 18 (62)

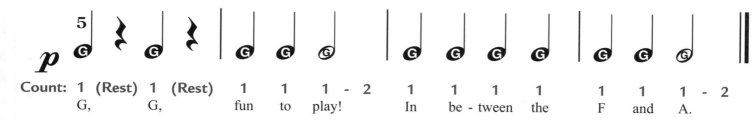

Count:	1	(Rest)	1	(Rest)	1	1	1 - 2	1	1	1	1	1	1	1 - 2
	G,		G,		fun	to	play!	In	be - tween	the		F	and	A.

49

$\frac{4}{4}$ Time Signature

The two numbers at the beginning of every piece are called a time signature.
The time signature tells you how many beats are in each measure.
The top number (4) tells you there are four beats in each measure.
The bottom number (4) means that a quarter note gets one beat.

Introducing the Page

Discuss the information on page 51 with your child.

Review C, D, E, F, and G on the keyboard. Then, play these five notes going up and down using the right hand. Begin with the thumb on C and place consecutive fingers on consecutive keys.

For each piece on the page, follow these steps:

1. Clap the rhythm of the piece. Each piece is in $\frac{4}{4}$ time.
2. "Play" the piece on the closed keyboard cover and say the finger numbers aloud.
3. Play the piece on the keyboard and count aloud.
4. Play and sing the words.

Practice Suggestions

1. Clap (or tap) and count aloud evenly.
2. Point to the notes and rests and count aloud evenly.
3. Say the finger numbers aloud while playing the notes in the air.
4. Play and say the finger numbers.
5. Play and say the note names.
6. Play and sing the words.

Subsequent Lessons

1. Play C-D-E-F-G with RH fingers 1-2-3-4-5 up and down the keyboard.
2. Review *Ice Cream* and *Music Stars!* as needed.
3. Play *Ice Cream* and *Music Stars!* with the CD.

Notes:

4/4 Time Signature

You know how many beats are in each measure by looking at the *time signature*, which is always at the beginning of the music.

4 means **four** beats to each measure.
4 means a **quarter note** ♩ gets one beat.

Practice Directions

1. Clap (or tap) and count aloud evenly.
2. Point to the notes and rests and count aloud evenly.
3. Say the finger numbers aloud while playing the notes in the air.
4. Play and say the finger numbers.
5. Play and say the note names.
6. Play and sing the words.

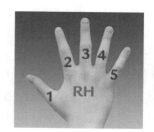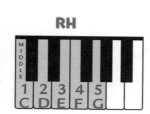

Ice Cream  Track 19 (63)

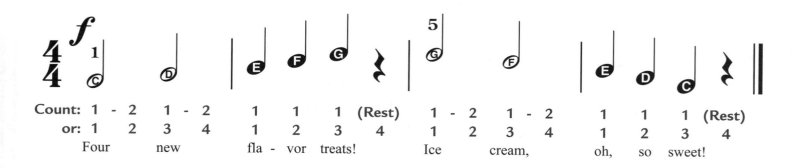

| Count: | 1 - 2 | 1 - 2 | 1 | 1 | 1 | (Rest) | 1 - 2 | 1 - 2 | 1 | 1 | 1 | (Rest) |
| or: | 1 | 2 | 3 | 4 | 1 | 2 | 3 | 4 | 1 | 2 | 3 | 4 | 1 | 2 | 3 | 4 |

Four new fla - vor treats! Ice cream, oh, so sweet!

Music Stars! Track 20 (64)

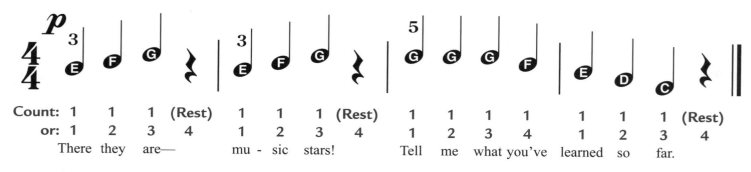

| Count: | 1 | 1 | 1 | (Rest) | 1 | 1 | 1 | (Rest) | 1 | 1 | 1 | 1 | 1 | 1 | 1 | (Rest) |
| or: | 1 | 2 | 3 | 4 | 1 | 2 | 3 | 4 | 1 | 2 | 3 | 4 | 1 | 2 | 3 | 4 |

There they are— mu - sic stars! Tell me what you've learned so far.

$\frac{3}{4}$ Time & Dotted Half Notes

In this new time signature, the top number (**3**) indicates that there are three beats in each measure. The bottom number (**4**) means that a quarter note gets one beat.

The new note on this page is the dotted half note. It gets three counts. The dot to the right of a note means to add half the value of the note to the full value. Since a half note gets two beats, the dot adds an extra beat and creates three beats for the dotted half note.

Introducing the Page

Discuss the information on page 53 with your child.

Review C-D-E on the keyboard. Then, play these three notes going up and down using the right hand. Begin with the thumb on C and place consecutive fingers on consecutive notes.

Review C-B-A-G-F on the keyboard. Then, play these five notes going down and up using the left hand. Begin with the thumb on C and place consecutive fingers on consecutive notes.

For each piece on the page, follow these steps:

1. Clap the rhythm of the piece. Each piece is in $\frac{3}{4}$ time.
2. "Play" the piece on the closed keyboard cover and say the finger numbers aloud.
3. Play the piece on the keyboard and count aloud.
4. Play and sing the words aloud.

Practice Suggestions

1. Clap (or tap) and count aloud evenly.
2. Point to the notes and count aloud evenly.
3. Say the finger numbers aloud while playing the notes in the air.
4. Play and say the finger numbers.
5. Play and say the note names.
6. Play and sing the words.

Subsequent Lessons

1. Play C-D-E with RH fingers 1-2-3 up and down the keyboard.
2. Play C-B-A-G-F with LH fingers 1-2-3-4-5 down and up the keyboard.
3. Review *Ready to Play* and *Play $\frac{3}{4}$ Time* as needed.
4. Play *Ready to Play* and *Play $\frac{3}{4}$ Time* with the CD.

Notes:

/4 Time & Dotted Half Notes

Introducing the Dotted Half Note

𝅗𝅥.

A *dotted half note* gets **three** counts. It looks like a half note with a dot to the right of the notehead.

𝅗𝅥.

Count: 1 - 2 - 3

3/4 means **three** beats to each measure.

means a **quarter note** ♩ gets one beat.

Practice Directions

1. Clap (or tap) and count aloud evenly.
2. Point to the notes and count aloud evenly.
3. Say the finger numbers aloud while playing the notes in the air.
4. Play and say the finger numbers.
5. Play and say the note names.
6. Play and sing the words.

Ready to Play Track 21 (65)

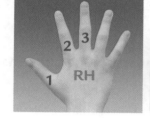
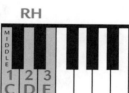

Count:	1 - 2 - 3	1 - 2 - 3	1	1	1	1 - 2 - 3	
or:	1 2 3	1 2 3	1	2	3	1 2 3	
	Now I	it's am	my read	les y	son to	day. play.	

Play 3/4 Time Track 22 (66)

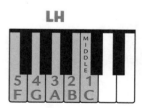
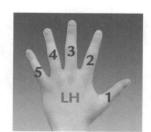

Count:	1 1 1	1 1 1	1 1 1	1 - 2 - 3			
or:	1 2 3	1 2 3	1 2 3	1 2 3			
	Three beats per It's so much	meas - ure, oh, fun when I	I'm do - ing play 3 - 4	fine. time.			

53

Moderately Loud Sounds

The sign *mf* stands for *mezzo forte*. This means to play moderately loud. Your child will use a medium amount of arm weight to play moderately loud.

Introducing the Page

Discuss the information on page 55 with your child.

1. Clap the rhythm of the piece. The piece is in 4/4 time.
2. "Play" the piece on the closed keyboard cover and say the finger numbers aloud.
3. Play the piece on the keyboard and count aloud.
4. Play and sing the words aloud.

Practice Suggestions

1. Clap (or tap) and count aloud evenly.
2. Point to the notes and count aloud evenly.
3. Say the finger numbers aloud while playing the notes in the air.
4. Play and say the finger numbers.
5. Play and say the note names.
6. Play and sing the words.

Subsequent Lessons

1. Play *Yankee Doodle* in different registers of the keyboard.
2. Play *Yankee Doodle* with the CD.

Notes:

Moderately Loud Sounds

mf

The sign *mf* stands for *mezzo forte*, which means to play **moderately loud**.

Practice Directions

1. Clap (or tap) and count aloud evenly.
2. Point to the notes and count aloud evenly.
3. Say the finger numbers aloud while playing the notes in the air.
4. Play and say the finger numbers.
5. Play and say the note names.
6. Play and sing the words.

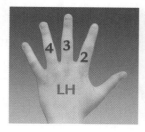
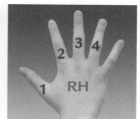

Yankee Doodle

Track 23 (67)

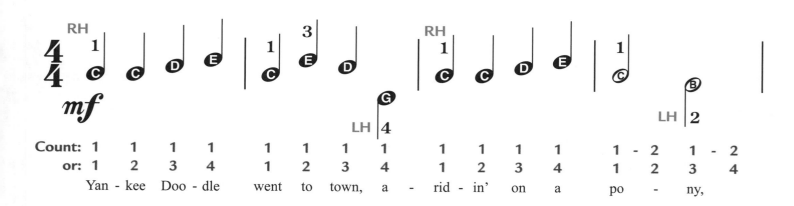

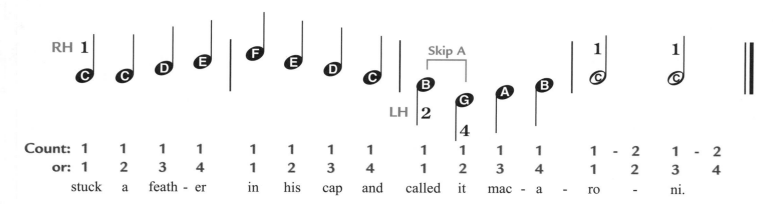

55

The Staff

Each note has a letter name. Notes are named by where they are placed on the staff. A staff is made up of five horizontal lines and the four spaces between those lines.

Notes written with lines going through them are said to be **on** the lines and are called line notes.

Notes written **in** the spaces are called space notes.

Introducing the Page

Discuss the information and complete the activities on page 57 with your child.

1. Point to the lines on the page and count them from bottom to top.
2. Point to the spaces on the page and count them from bottom to top.
3. Point to each note on the page and name it as a line note or a space note.

Practice Directions

1. Take a blank piece of paper and draw three staffs.
2. On the first staff, number the lines from bottom to top. Then, number the spaces from bottom to top.
3. On the second staff, practice drawing space notes.
4. On the third staff, practice drawing line notes.

Subsequent Lessons

Review the staff as needed.

Notes:

The Staff

Each note has a name. That name depends on where the note is found on the *staff*.
The staff is made up of five horizontal lines and the spaces between those lines.

Line Notes on the Staff

The staff has **five lines.**

Notes can be written **on** the lines.

Draw a red circle around each line note.

Space Notes on the Staff

The staff has **four spaces.**

Notes can be written **in** the spaces.

Draw a blue circle around each space note.

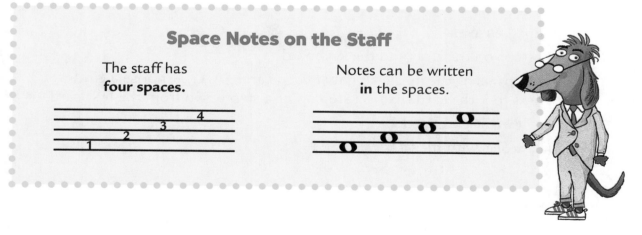

Treble Clef

Clef signs are symbols that have evolved over hundreds of years of music history. These symbols are used as reference points for all other notes.
The *Treble Clef* sign indicates notes that usually are played with the right hand.

Introducing the Page

Discuss the information on page 59 with your child.

Extra lines can be added to the staff so that additional notes can be written. Middle C is written on the first leger line below the treble staff.
Trace the Treble Clef sign and the Middle C on the page.

One note above Middle C is Treble D. It is written on the space below the first line.

The distance from Middle C to D is called a step. Steps on the staff are written from a line to a space or a space to a line. On the keyboard, one white key up or down to the next is a step.

For *Take a Step,* follow these steps:

1. Point to the notes in the piece. Ask your child to name the notes.
2. Clap the rhythm of the piece. The piece is in $\frac{3}{4}$ time.
3. "Play" the piece on the closed keyboard cover and say the finger numbers aloud.
4. Play the piece on the keyboard and count aloud.
5. Play and sing the words.

Practice Directions

1. Clap (or tap) and count aloud evenly.
2. Point to the notes and count aloud evenly.
3. Say the finger numbers aloud while playing the notes in the air.
4. Play and say the finger numbers.
5. Play and say the note names.
6. Play and sing the words.

Subsequent Lessons

1. Review steps on the staff and the keyboard.
2. Review steps using the music alphabet flash cards (A–G). Choose a card. Place next to it the card that is a step up or a step down from the first card.
3. Review *Take a Step* as needed.
4. Play *Take a Step* with the CD.

Notes:

Treble Clef

As music notation progressed through history, the staff had 2 to 20 lines. Symbols were invented that would always give a reference point for all other notes. These symbols are called *clefs*.

Introducing the Treble Clef

Play *treble clef* notes with the right hand.

Treble Clef

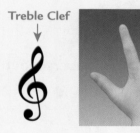

Steps

From one white key to the next, up or down, is a *step*.

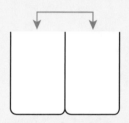

Steps are written **line to space** or **space to line.**

Treble Clef Middle C

Middle C is the C nearest the middle of the piano keyboard.

Treble Clef D

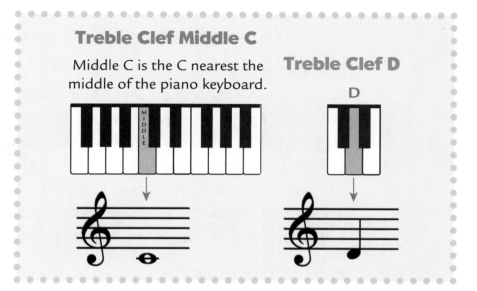

Activity

Trace the treble clef with a black crayon, and trace the middle C with a green crayon.

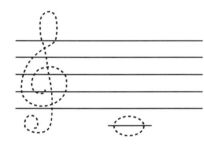

Practice Directions

"Take a Step" uses repeated notes and steps up and down.

1. Clap (or tap) and count aloud evenly.
2. Point to the notes and count aloud evenly.
3. Say the finger numbers aloud while playing the notes in the air.
4. Play and say the finger numbers.
5. Play and say the note names.
6. Play and sing the words.

Take a Step

 Track 24 (68)

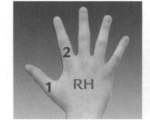

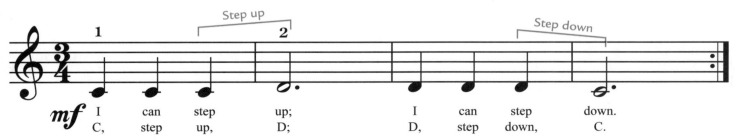

mf

| I | can | step | up; | | I | can | step | down. |
| C, | step | up, | D; | | D, | step | down, | C. |

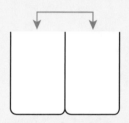

Treble Clef E

Treble E is one step above Treble D. It is written on the first line of the treble staff.

Treble Clef F and Treble Clef G

If you continue stepping up on the staff, you will find Treble Clef F and Treble Clef G. Treble Clef F is in the first space and is one step up from Treble Clef E. Treble Clef G is on the second line and is one step up from Treble Clef F.

Introducing the Page

Discuss the information on page 61 with your child.

For each piece on the page, follow these steps:

1. Point to the notes in the piece. Ask your child to name the notes.
2. Clap the rhythm of the piece.
3. "Play" the piece on the closed keyboard cover and say the finger numbers aloud.
4. Play the piece on the keyboard and count aloud.
5. Play and sing the words.

Practice Directions

1. Clap (or tap) and count aloud evenly.
2. Point to the notes and count aloud evenly.
3. Say the finger numbers aloud while playing the notes in the air.
4. Play and say the finger numbers.
5. Play and say the note names.
6. Play and sing the words.

Subsequent Lessons

1. Review steps on the staff and the keyboard.
2. Review the music alphabet.
3. Review notes in the treble staff from Middle C up to Treble G.
4. Review *Stepping Fun* and *Right Hand Song* as needed.
5. Play *Stepping Fun* and *Right Hand Song* with the CD.

Notes:

Practice Directions

1. Clap (or tap) and count aloud evenly.
2. Point to the notes and count aloud evenly.
3. Say the finger numbers aloud while playing the notes in the air.
4. Play and say the finger numbers.
5. Play and say the note names.
6. Play and sing the words.

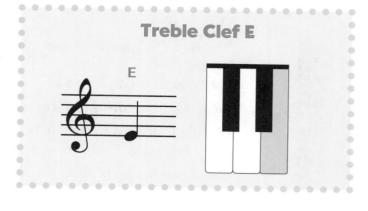

Stepping Fun  Track 25 (69)

Circle the repeated notes in "Stepping Fun." All other notes are steps.

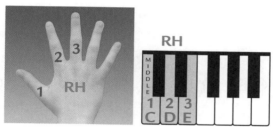

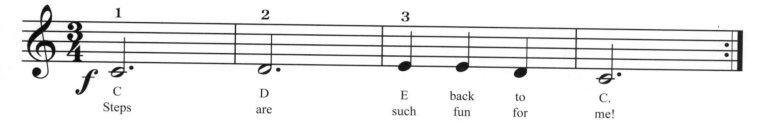

| C | D | E | back | to | C. |
| Steps | are | such | fun | for | me! |

Right Hand Song  Track 26 (70)

This piece uses all five fingers of the right hand.

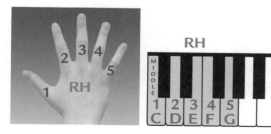

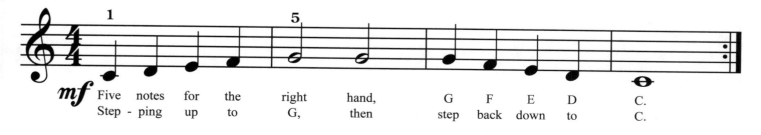

| Five | notes | for | the | right | hand, | | G | F | E | D | C. |
| Step - | ping | up | to | G, | then | | step | back | down | to | C. |

Bass Clef

The *Bass Clef* sign indicates notes that usually are played with the left hand.

Introducing the Page

Discuss the information on page 63 with your child.

Middle C is written on the first leger line above the bass staff.
Trace the Bass Clef sign and the Middle C on the page.

One note below Middle C is B. It is written on the space above the top line.

For *Stepping Down,* follow these steps:

1. Point to the notes in the piece. Ask your child to name the notes.
2. Clap the rhythm of the piece. The piece is in $\frac{4}{4}$ time.
3. "Play" the piece on the closed keyboard cover and say the finger numbers aloud.
4. Play the piece on the keyboard and count aloud.
5. Play and sing the words.

Practice Directions

1. Clap (or tap) and count aloud evenly.
2. Point to the notes and rests and count aloud evenly.
3. Say the finger numbers aloud while playing the notes in the air.
4. Play and say the finger numbers.
5. Play and say the note names.
6. Play and sing the words.

Subsequent Lessons

1. Review steps on the staff and the keyboard.
2. Review steps in the music alphabet.
3. Review *Stepping Down* as needed.
4. Play *Stepping Down* with the CD.

Notes:

Bass Clef

Introducing the Bass Clef

Play *bass clef* notes with the left hand.

Bass Clef

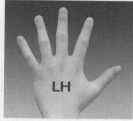
LH

Bass Clef Middle C

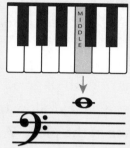

Bass Clef B

Activity

Trace the bass clef with a black crayon, and trace the middle C with a green crayon.

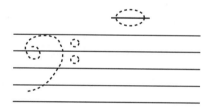

Practice Directions

Measures 2 and 4 of this song use repeated notes.

1. Clap (or tap) and count aloud evenly.
2. Point to the notes and rests and count aloud evenly.
3. Say the finger numbers aloud while playing the notes in the air.

4. Play and say the finger numbers.
5. Play and say the note names.
6. Play and sing the words.

Stepping Down  Track 27 (71)

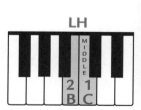
LH
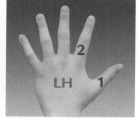
LH

mf

Step - ping down from mid - dle C, C, B, look at me!
There's so much that I can do. Step down, so can you.

63

Bass Clef A

Bass Clef A is one step below Bass Clef B.
It is written on the top line of the bass staff.

Bass Clef G and Bass Clef F

If you continue stepping down on the staff, you will find Bass Clef G and Bass Clef F. Bass Clef G is in the fourth space and is one step down from Bass Clef A. Bass Clef F is on the fourth line and is one step down from Bass Clef G.

Introducing the Page

Discuss the information on page 65 with your child.

For each piece on the page, follow these steps:

1. Point to the notes in the piece. Ask your child to name the notes.
2. Clap the rhythm of the piece.
3. "Play" the piece on the closed keyboard cover and say the finger numbers aloud.
4. Play the piece on the keyboard and count aloud.
5. Play and sing the words.

Practice Directions

1. Clap (or tap) and count aloud evenly.
2. Point to the notes and count aloud evenly.
3. Say the finger numbers aloud while playing the notes in the air.
4. Play and say the finger numbers.
5. Play and say the note names.
6. Play and sing the words.

Subsequent Lessons

1. Review steps on the staff and the keyboard.
2. Review steps with the music alphabet flash cards.
3. Review notes in the bass staff from Middle C down to Bass Clef F.
4. Review *Music to Share* and *Left Hand Song*.
5. Play *Music to Share* and *Left Hand Song* with the CD.

Notes:

Practice Directions

1. Clap (or tap) and count aloud evenly.
2. Point to the notes and count aloud evenly.
3. Say the finger numbers aloud while playing the notes in the air.
4. Play and say the finger numbers.
5. Play and say the note names.
6. Play and sing the words.

Bass Clef A

Music to Share

Track 28 (72)

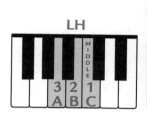
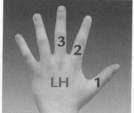

Circle the repeated notes in "Music to Share." All other notes are steps.

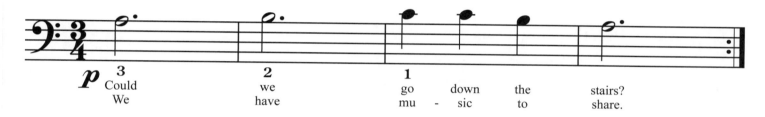

p

3	2	1			
Could	we	go	down	the	stairs?
We	have	mu - sic	to	share.	

Bass Clef G

Bass Clef F

Left Hand Song

Track 29 (73)

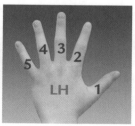

This song uses all five fingers of the left hand.

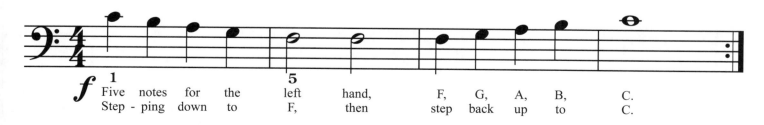

f

1				5						
Five	notes	for	the	left	hand,	F,	G,	A,	B,	C.
Step - ping	down	to	F,	then	step	back	up	to	C.	

Skips

When you skip a white key and a finger, you are playing a skip.
On the staff, skips are written from a line to a line or a space to a space.

Introducing the Page

Discuss the information on page 67 with your child.

Use the music alphabet flash cards to introduce skips. Choose a card.
Place next to it the card that is a skip up or a skip down from the first card.

Find skips on the keyboard. Name the keys as they are played.

Circle the skips in *Music Friend* and *Circle Time*.

For each piece on the page, follow these steps:

1. Point to the notes in the piece. Ask your child to name the notes.
2. Clap the rhythm of the piece. The pieces are in $\frac{4}{4}$ time.
3. "Play" the piece on the closed keyboard cover and say the finger numbers aloud.
4. Play the piece on the keyboard and count aloud.
5. Play and sing the words.

Practice Directions

1. Clap (or tap) and count aloud evenly.
2. Point to the notes and rests and count aloud evenly.
3. Say the finger numbers aloud while playing the notes in the air.
4. Play and say the finger numbers.
5. Play and say the note names.
6. Play and sing the words.

Subsequent Lessons

1. Review skips on the staff and the keyboard.
2. Review skips using the music alphabet flash cards.
3. Review *Music Friend* and *Circle Time* as needed.
4. Play *Music Friend* and *Circle Time* with the CD.

Notes:

Practice Directions

1. Clap (or tap) and count aloud evenly.
2. Point to the notes and rests and count aloud evenly.
3. Say the finger numbers aloud while playing the notes in the air.
4. Play and say the finger numbers.
5. Play and say the note names.
6. Play and sing the words.

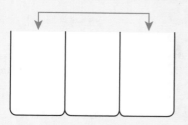

Skips

When you skip over a white key, you also skip a finger.

Skips are written **line to line** or **space to space**.

Music Friend Track 30 (74)

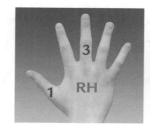
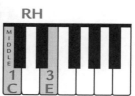

Measure 3 of "Music Friend" uses repeated notes.

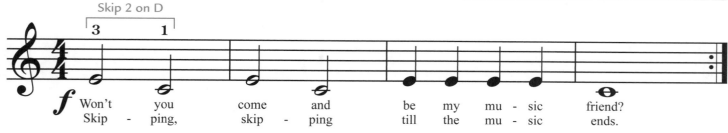

Won't you come and be my mu - sic friend?
Skip - ping, skip - ping till the mu - sic ends.

Circle Time Track 31 (75)

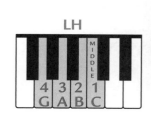
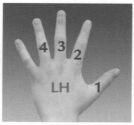

Find and circle the two steps in "Circle Time."

Cir - cling skips can sure be fun! In this piece, there's more than one.
Grab a cray - on, skip to B. Find - ing skips is fun for me!

The Grand Staff

The Grand Staff is created by joining the treble staff and bass staff together with a *brace*. The grand staff is used to show notes for both the right and left hand. A *leger line* between the staffs is used for Middle C.

Middle C Position on the Grand Staff

When placing both thumbs on Middle C and placing consecutive fingers on consecutive keys, the hands are in Middle C Position.

The thumbs share the same note—Middle C. Review finding Middle C just below the center two-black-key group.

Introducing the Page

Discuss the information on page 69 with your child.

1. Place both thumbs on Middle C.
2. Place the remaining right-hand fingers on D, E, F, and G.
3. Place the remaining left-hand fingers on B, A, G, and F.
4. Point to the notes on the staff and have your child name and play them while the hands are in Middle C position.

Practice Directions

Practice naming and playing the notes on the staff.

Subsequent Lessons

1. Review the notes as needed.
2. Review steps and skips with the music alphabet flash cards.

Notes:

The Grand Staff

When the treble staff and bass staff are joined together with a *brace,* it is called the *grand staff.* The grand staff is used to show notes for both the right and left hands.

A short line between the two staffs is used for **middle C.**

Brace

Middle C Position on the Grand Staff

When playing in middle C position, either thumb can play middle C.

Just for You

This is the first piece that is written on the grand staff.
Just for You is written in Middle C position and uses steps, skips, and repeated notes.

Introducing the Page

1. Point to the notes in *Just for You* and have your child name them.
2. Put the hands in Middle C position.
   Point to each note and have your child name and play it.
3. Clap and count the rhythm aloud.
4. Play and name the steps, skips, and repeats.
5. Play and name the notes.
6. Play and sing the words.

Practice Directions

1. Clap (or tap) and count aloud evenly.
2. Point to the notes and rests and count aloud evenly.
3. Say the finger numbers aloud while playing the notes in the air.
4. Play and say the finger numbers.
5. Play and say the note names.
6. Play and sing the words.

Subsequent Lessons

1. Review the notes on the staff.
2. Review steps and skips with the music alphabet flash cards.
3. Review *Just for You* as needed.
4. Play *Just for You* with the CD.

Notes:

Practice Directions

1. Clap (or tap) and count aloud evenly.
2. Point to the notes and rests and count aloud evenly.
3. Say the finger numbers aloud while playing the notes in the air.
4. Play and say the finger numbers.
5. Play and say the note names.
6. Play and sing the words.

Just for You  Track 32 (76)

Both hands of "Just for You" play steps, skips, and repeated notes.

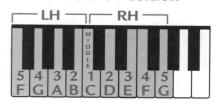

Middle C Position

LH ─── RH

5 4 3 2 1 2 3 4 5
F G A B C D E F G

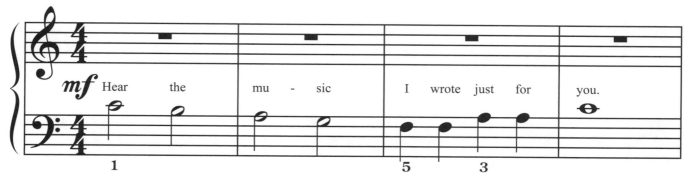

mf Hear the mu - sic I wrote just for you.

1   5   3

5

1   5   3

Now you know I think you're spe - cial, too!

Half Rest

A half rest is the corresponding rest to the half note. It gets two counts and means to rest for two beats. Your child will count this rest saying "rest – 2." He or she will clap on the word "rest" and then turn the palms up for count "2."

Introducing the Page

Discuss the information on page 73 with your child.

Haydn's Symphony is written in Middle C Position and uses steps, skips, and repeated notes.

For *Haydn's Symphony,* follow these steps:

1. Clap the rhythm and count aloud. For the half rest, have your child clap on the word "rest" and then turn the palms up for count "2."
2. "Play" the piece on the closed keyboard cover and say the finger numbers aloud. For the half rest, have your child lift the finger off the closed keyboard.
3. Play the piece on the keyboard and count aloud. For the half rest, have your child lift the finger off the keyboard.
4. Play the piece and name the notes.
5. Play and sing the words.

Practice Directions

1. Clap (or tap) and count aloud evenly.
2. Point to the notes and rests and count aloud evenly.
3. Say the finger numbers aloud while playing the notes in the air.
4. Play and say the finger numbers.
5. Play and say the note names.
6. Play and sing the words.

Subsequent Lessons

1. Review *Haydn's Symphony* as needed.
2. Play *Haydn's Symphony* with the CD.

Notes:

Half Rest

Practice Directions

1. Clap (or tap) and count aloud evenly.
2. Point to the notes and rests and count aloud evenly.
3. Say the finger numbers aloud while playing the notes in the air.
4. Play and say the finger numbers.
5. Play and say the note names.
6. Play and sing the words.

Introducing the Half Rest

A *half rest* gets **two** counts. Do not play for two counts, which is the same as two quarter notes.

Count: Rest - 2
Or: 1 - 2

Haydn's Symphony

Middle C Position

Track 33 (77)

Franz Joseph Haydn

mf Hay - dn wrote a sym - pho - ny. I will play it beau - ti - f'ly.

All my friends will want to be in the or - ches - tra with me.

73

London Bridge

London Bridge is written in Middle C Position.
Notice that both hands begin with finger 2.

Introducing the Page

For *London Bridge,* follow these steps:

1. Clap the rhythm and count aloud. For the half rest, have your child turn the palms up for the two counts.
2. "Play" the piece on the closed keyboard cover and say the finger numbers aloud.
3. Play the piece on the keyboard and count aloud.
4. Play the piece and name the notes.
5. Play and sing the words.

Practice Directions

1. Clap (or tap) and count aloud evenly.
2. Point to the notes and rests and count aloud evenly.
3. Say the finger numbers aloud while playing the notes in the air.
4. Play and say the finger numbers.
5. Play and say the note names.
6. Play and sing the words.

Subsequent Lessons

1. Review *London Bridge* as needed.
2. Play *London Bridge* with the CD.

Notes:

Practice Directions

1. Clap (or tap) and count aloud evenly.
2. Point to the notes and rests and count aloud evenly.
3. Say the finger numbers aloud while playing the notes in the air.
4. Play and say the finger numbers.
5. Play and say the note names.
6. Play and sing the words.

London Bridge  Track 34 (78)

Middle C Position

Notice that both hands begin with finger 2 for this piece.

Twinkle, Twinkle, Little Star

Twinkle, Twinkle, Little Star is written in Middle C position. Notice that the left hand begins with finger 4, and the right hand begins with finger 2.

Introducing the Page

For *Twinkle, Twinkle, Little Star,* follow these steps:

1. Clap the rhythm and count aloud.
2. "Play" the piece on the closed keyboard cover and say the finger numbers aloud.
3. Play the piece on the keyboard and count aloud.
4. Play the piece and name the notes.
5. Play and sing the words.

Practice Directions

1. Clap (or tap) and count aloud evenly.
2. Point to the notes and rests and count aloud evenly.
3. Say the finger numbers aloud while playing the notes in the air.
4. Play and say the finger numbers.
5. Play and say the note names.
6. Play and sing the words.

Subsequent Lessons

1. Review *Twinkle, Twinkle, Little Star* as needed.
2. Play *Twinkle, Twinkle, Little Star* with the CD.

Notes:

Practice Directions

1. Clap (or tap) and count aloud evenly.
2. Point to the notes and rests and count aloud evenly.
3. Say the finger numbers aloud while playing the notes in the air.
4. Play and say the finger numbers.
5. Play and say the note names.
6. Play and sing the words.

Twinkle, Twinkle, Little Star

Middle C Position

 Track 35 (79)

77

Jingle Bells

Jingle Bells is written in Middle C Position.
Notice that each hand begins with finger 2.

Introducing the Page

For *Jingle Bells,* follow these steps:

1. Clap the rhythm and count aloud.
2. "Play" the piece on the closed keyboard cover and say the finger numbers aloud.
3. Play the piece on the keyboard and count aloud.
4. Play the piece and name the notes.
5. Play and sing the words.

Practice Directions

1. Clap (or tap) and count aloud evenly.
2. Point to the notes and rests and count aloud evenly.
3. Say the finger numbers aloud while playing the notes in the air.
4. Play and say the finger numbers.
5. Play and say the note names.
6. Play and sing the words.

Subsequent Lessons

1. Review *Jingle Bells* as needed.
2. Play *Jingle Bells* with the CD.

Notes:

Practice Directions

1. Clap (or tap) and count aloud evenly.
2. Point to the notes and rests and count aloud evenly.
3. Say the finger numbers aloud while playing the notes in the air.
4. Play and say the finger numbers.
5. Play and say the note names.
6. Play and sing the words.

Jingle Bells

Middle C Position

 Track 36 (80)

James S. Pierpont

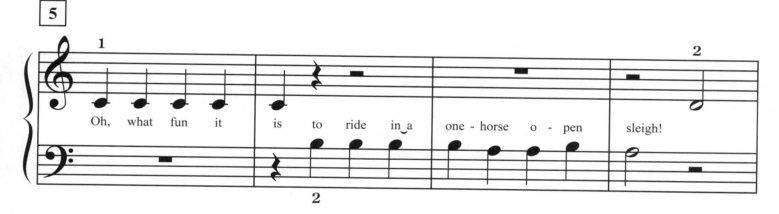

Jin - gle bells! Jin - gle bells! Jin - gle all the way!

Oh, what fun it is to ride in a one - horse o - pen sleigh!

Jin - gle bells! Jin - gle bells! Jin - gle all the way!

Oh, what fun it is to ride in a one - horse o - pen sleigh!

79

Bass Clef C and Bass Clef D

Bass Clef C is the C below Middle C. It is written in the second space.
Bass D is next to Bass Clef C. It is written on the third line.

Introducing the Page

Find Bass Clef C on the keyboard and the staff.

Name the notes in *New C*. For *New C*, follow the practice directions below.

Find Bass Clef D on the keyboard and the staff.

Name the notes in *Three "D"-lightful Friends*.
For *Three "D"-lightful Friends*, follow the practice directions below.

Practice Directions

1. Clap (or tap) and count aloud evenly.
2. Point to the notes and rests and count aloud evenly.
3. Say the finger numbers aloud while playing the notes in the air.
4. Play and say the finger numbers.
5. Play and say the note names.
6. Play and sing the words.

Subsequent Lessons

1. Review Bass Clef C and Bass Clef D on the staff and keyboard.
2. Review *New C* and *Three "D"-lightful Friends* as needed.
3. Play *New C* and *Three "D"-lightful Friends* with the CD.

Notes:

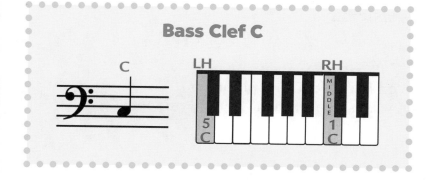

Practice Directions

1. Clap (or tap) and count aloud evenly.
2. Point to the notes and rests and count aloud evenly.
3. Say the finger numbers aloud while playing the notes in the air.
4. Play and say the finger numbers.
5. Play and say the note names.
6. Play and sing the words.

New C   Track 37 (81)

Both hands play C.

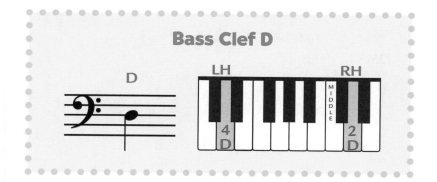

Three "D"-lightful Friends   Track 38 (82)

Both hands play D.

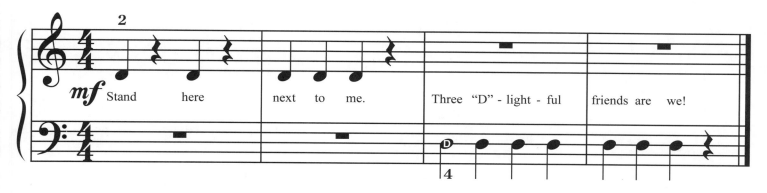

Bass Clef E, F and G in C Position

Bass Clef E is the E below Middle C. It is written in the second space. F and G in C Position are the two notes above E.

When placing left-hand finger 5 on Bass Clef C and placing consecutive fingers on consecutive keys, the left hand is in C Position.

Introducing the Page

Find Bass Clef E on the keyboard and the staff.

Name the notes in *Finger 3 on E*. For *Finger 3 on E,* follow the practice directions below.

Find Bass Clef F and Bass Clef G on the keyboard and the staff.

Name the notes in *Great Big Day*. For *Great Big Day,* follow the practice directions below.

Practice Directions

1. Clap (or tap) and count aloud evenly.
2. Point to the notes and rests and count aloud evenly.
3. Say the finger numbers aloud while playing the notes in the air.
4. Play and say the finger numbers.
5. Play and say the note names.
6. Play and sing the words.

Subsequent Lessons

1. Review Bass Clef E, F, and G on the staff and keyboard.
2. Review *Finger 3 on E* and *Great Big Day* as needed.
3. Play *Finger 3 on E* and *Great Big Day* with the CD.

Notes:

Bass Clef E

Practice Directions

1. Clap (or tap) and count aloud evenly.
2. Point to the notes and rests and count aloud evenly.
3. Say the finger numbers aloud while playing the notes in the air.
4. Play and say the finger numbers.
5. Play and say the note names.
6. Play and sing the words.

Finger 3 on E ● Track 39 (83)

Both hands play E.

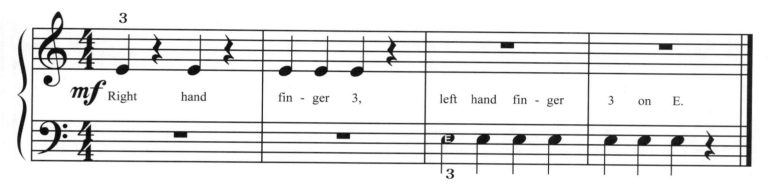

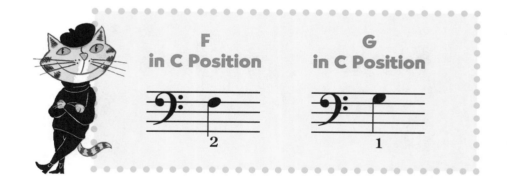

F in C Position

G in C Position

Great Big Day ● Track 40 (84)

C Position

C Position for LH

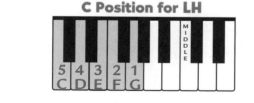

This piece uses all five fingers of the left hand.

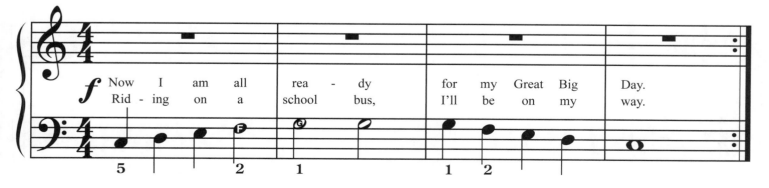

C Position on the Grand Staff

C Position on the Grand Staff uses the notes C, D, E, F, and G in the treble and bass clefs. To play in this position, the right-hand thumb is on Middle C and the left-hand fifth finger is on Bass Clef C.

Introducing the Page

Point to and name the notes in C position on the Grand Staff.

Point to and name the notes in *Ode to Joy.*
For *Ode to Joy,* follow the practice directions below.

Practice Directions

1. Clap (or tap) and count aloud evenly.
2. Point to the notes and rests and count aloud evenly.
3. Say the finger numbers aloud while playing the notes in the air.
4. Play and say the finger numbers.
5. Play and say the note names.
6. Play and sing the words.

Subsequent Lessons

1. Review C Position on the staff and keyboard.
2. Review *Ode to Joy* as needed.
3. Play *Ode to Joy* with the CD.

Notes:

C Position on the Grand Staff

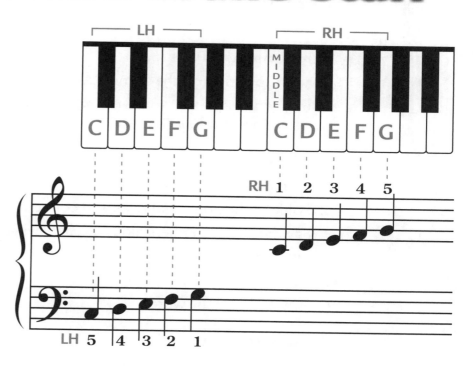

Practice Directions

1. Clap (or tap) and count aloud evenly.
2. Point to the notes and rests and count aloud evenly.
3. Say the finger numbers aloud while playing the notes in the air.
4. Play and say the finger numbers.
5. Play and say the note names.
6. Play and sing the words.

Ode to Joy

(Theme from the Ninth Symphony)

 Track 41 (85)

Both hands begin with finger 3 on E.

Ludwig van Beethoven

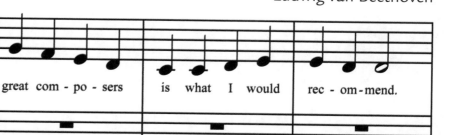

mf Mu - sic by the great com - po - sers is what I would rec - om - mend.

When I play Bee - tho - ven's mu - sic, I wish it would nev - er end.

Row, Row, Row Your Boat

Row, Row, Row Your Boat uses the C Position in each hand.
Each hand begins with finger 1.

Introducing the Page

Review C position on the grand staff.

Point to and name the notes in *Row, Row, Row Your Boat.*
For *Row, Row, Row Your Boat,* follow the practice directions below.

Practice Directions

1. Clap (or tap) and count aloud evenly.
2. Point to the notes and rests and count aloud evenly.
3. Say the finger numbers aloud while playing the notes in the air.
4. Play and say the finger numbers.
5. Play and say the note names.
6. Play and sing the words.

Subsequent Lessons

1. Review C Position on the staff and keyboard.
2. Review *Row, Row, Row Your Boat* as needed.
3. Play *Row, Row, Row Your Boat* with the CD.

Notes:

1. Clap (or tap) and count aloud evenly.
2. Point to the notes and rests and count aloud evenly.
3. Say the finger numbers aloud while playing the notes in the air.
4. Play and say the finger numbers.
5. Play and say the note names.
6. Play and sing the words.

Row, Row, Row Your Boat

C Position Track 42 (86)

A whole rest gets three beats in $\frac{3}{4}$ time.

Hush, Little Baby

Hush, Little Baby uses the C Position in each hand.
The left hand begins with finger 1, and the right hand begins with finger 3.

Introducing the Page

Review C position on the grand staff.

Point to and name the notes in *Hush, Little Baby*.
For *Hush, Little Baby*, follow the practice directions below.

Practice Directions

1. Clap (or tap) and count aloud evenly.
2. Point to the notes and rests and count aloud evenly.
3. Say the finger numbers aloud while playing the notes in the air.
4. Play and say the finger numbers.
5. Play and say the note names.
6. Play and sing the words.

Subsequent Lessons

1. Review C Position on the staff and keyboard.
2. Review *Hush, Little Baby* as needed.
3. Play *Hush, Little Baby* with the CD.

Notes:

1. Clap (or tap) and count aloud evenly.
2. Point to the notes and rests and count aloud evenly.
3. Say the finger numbers aloud while playing the notes in the air.
4. Play and say the finger numbers.
5. Play and say the note names.
6. Play and sing the words.

Hush, Little Baby

C Position  Track 43 (87)

Each line begins with the left hand and changes to the right.

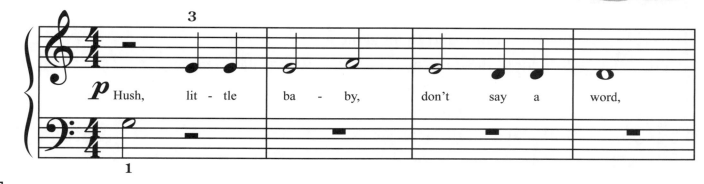

Hush, lit - tle ba - by, don't say a word,

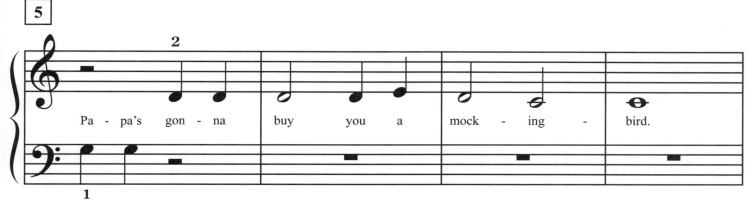

Pa - pa's gon - na buy you a mock - ing - bird.

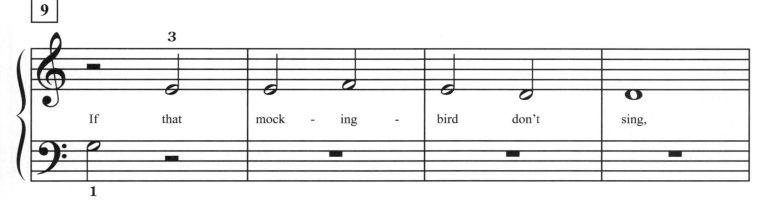

If that mock - ing - bird don't sing,

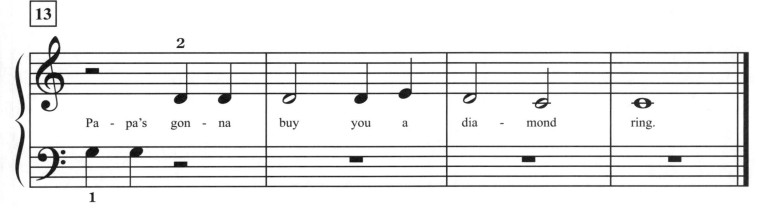

Pa - pa's gon - na buy you a dia - mond ring.

The Wheels on the Bus

The Wheels on the Bus uses the C Position in each hand.
Each hand begins with finger 1.

Introducing the Page

Review C position on the grand staff.

Point to and name the notes in *The Wheels on the Bus*.
For *The Wheels on the Bus,* follow the practice directions below.

Practice Directions

1. Clap (or tap) and count aloud evenly.
2. Point to the notes and rests and count aloud evenly.
3. Say the finger numbers aloud while playing the notes in the air.
4. Play and say the finger numbers.
5. Play and say the note names.
6. Play and sing the words.

Subsequent Lessons

1. Review C Position on the staff and keyboard.
2. Review *The Wheels on the Bus* as needed.
3. Play *The Wheels on the Bus* with the CD.

Notes:

Practice Directions

1. Clap (or tap) and count aloud evenly.
2. Point to the notes and rests and count aloud evenly.
3. Say the finger numbers aloud while playing the notes in the air.
4. Play and say the finger numbers.
5. Play and say the note names.
6. Play and sing the words.

The Wheels on the Bus

C Position Track 44 (88)

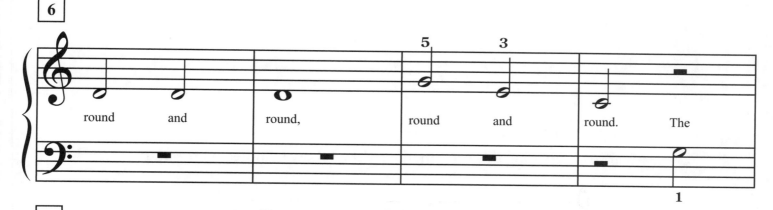

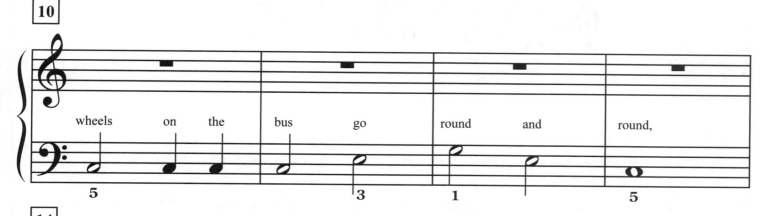

91

Music Matching Game

Complete page 93 with your child in the lesson one section at a time. Check the answers using the answer key.

Symbols

Notes:

Rests:

Dynamic Signs: *p* *mf* *f*

Time Signatures: $\frac{3}{4}$ $\frac{4}{4}$

Repeat Sign:

Treble Clef Notes

Before completing this section, review the following notes on the staff:

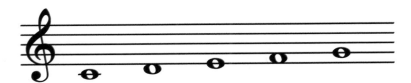

Bass Clef Notes

Before completing this section, review the following notes on the staff:

Music Matching Game

Symbols

Draw a line to match each symbol on the left to its name on the right.

1. ♩   repeat sign
2. $\frac{3}{4}$ moderately loud
3. :‖   three beats in each measure
4. *mf*   quarter rest
5. ▬   quarter note
6. 𝐨   loud
7. 𝄽   four beats in each measure
8. *f*   dotted half note
9. ♩   whole note
10. *p*   half rest
11. $\frac{4}{4}$ half note
12. ▬   whole rest
13. ♩.   soft

Treble Clef Notes

Draw a line to match each treble clef note on the left to its correct letter name on the right.

1.   C
2.   D
3.   E
4.   F
5.   G

Bass Clef Notes

Draw a line to match each bass clef note on the left to its correct letter name on the right.

1.   C
2.   D
3.   E
4.   F
5.   G
6.   A
7.   B

Answer Key

Treble Clef Notes
1. G
2. D
3. C
4. E
5. F

Bass Clef Notes
1. D
2. G
3. C
4. B
5. A
6. F
7. E

Symbols
1. quarter note
2. three beats in each measure
3. repeat sign
4. moderately loud
5. half rest
6. whole note
7. quarter rest
8. loud
9. half note
10. soft
11. four beats in each measure
12. whole rest
13. dotted half note

Parent Guide

Certificate of Completion

Complete the certificate in the lesson and congratulate your child.

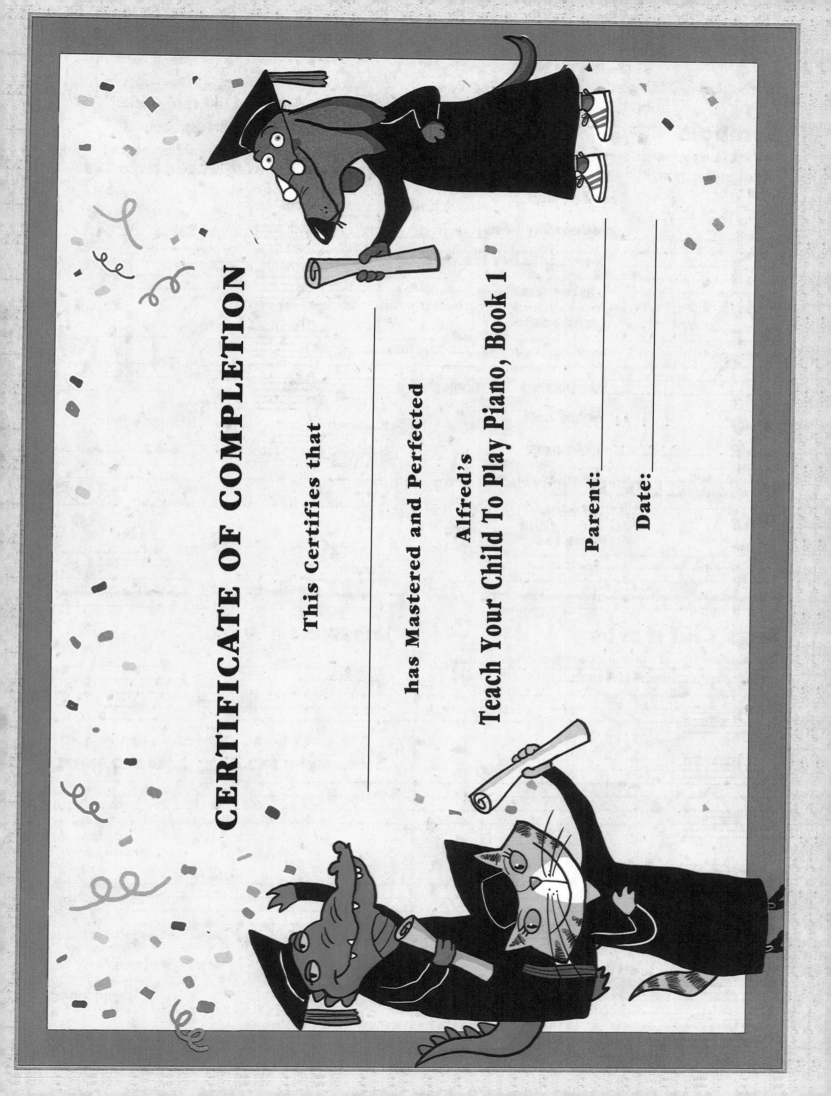

CERTIFICATE OF COMPLETION

This Certifies that

_____

has Mastered and Perfected

Alfred's
Teach Your Child To Play Piano, Book 1

Parent: _____

Date: _____

Frequently Asked Questions

How long should lessons last and how frequently should they occur?

Lessons should be held once or twice a week and will typically last from 30 to 45 minutes. Another workable scenario is to practice daily with your child, structuring each "practice" to introduce new material as well.

How much material should be covered in each lesson?

The amount of material covered in each lesson will vary. This is gauged by how well your child plays the pieces that have been assigned, how long it takes to review them, and how long it takes to introduce a new piece.

How long should a student continue with each piece?

Students should practice each piece until it can be played at the appropriate tempo without stopping while following all of the musical markings. An excellent way to judge the proficiency of each piece is to play it with the CD. If your child cannot play the piece with the CD without stopping, then more time probably is needed on that piece. However, staying on any one piece for too long a period of time can be discouraging to your child.

What should I do when my child finishes this book?

You may want to consider finding a professional piano teacher for your child at this point.